CHOSEN FOREVER

CHOSEN FOREVER

· A MEMOIR ·

xo

SUSAN RICHARDS

To my dear Pat,
It's wonderful.
See your smiling
face at readings.
Thank you & love,
Susan Richards

SOHO

Correspondence on pages 70-71, 157, 160, 169-170, 197, 202-203, 219, 220 reprinted by permission of Dennis Stock.

Correspondence on pages 181-184, reprinted by permission of Mary Wilson Williams.

Photograph on page 137 courtesy of Dennis Stock.

Photograph on page 275 courtesy of Andrea Barrett Stern.

Translation of *The Canticle of the Sun* by permission of Bill Barrett.

Published by Soho Press, Inc.
853 Broadway
New York, NY 10003

Library of Congress Cataloging-in-Publication Data
Richards, Susan. 1949–
Chosen forever : a memoir / Susan Richards.
     p. cm.
ISBN 978-1-56947-492-1 (hardcover)
1. Richards, Susan, 1949–
2. Authors, American—20th century—Biography.   I. Title.
PS3618.I34453Z46 2008
818'.603—dc22
[B]
2007042568

10   9   8   7   6   5   4   3   2   1

With love, to Dennis

Lay Me Down.

PREFACE

WINTERS CAN FEEL endless and gray when you live alone on a farm in upstate New York, and the winter of 2005 was the worst. I'd owned my home for twenty-four years and had spent the last ten trying to earn a living teaching as an adjunct in a nearby college, while at the same time devoting myself to a lifelong dream, writing. After completing two novels and a memoir, I remained unpublished. I'd had three agents, but had not sold a book. I was a fifty-five-year-old single woman facing a professional and financial crisis. I couldn't support myself on an adjunct's salary and I could no longer afford to spend time writing books that didn't sell. I was depressed and full of fears about the future. Then my memoir, about a racehorse named Lay Me Down that I had adopted, was accepted for publication.

I had no idea, on the raw, rainy day years earlier when Lay Me Down hobbled into my life, of the extent to which my future had just been changed. In an uncharacteristic moment, I had responded to an SPCA appeal and offered to take in one of more than forty Standardbred horses rescued from an abusive owner. I had selected a horse by the name of Current Squeeze from a list on which she was number 10. As I confronted the milling herd of frightened mares and foals in the paddock and attempted to locate the brass tag that bore the number 10 hanging from the cheek latch of one of their worn-out halters, a sick, emaciated bay mare followed by her foal walked up the ramp to my trailer of her own volition. This was Lay Me Down. I took her home to join the three horses I already had and things were never the same again.

During the years that she lived on my farm, her gentle, loving nature helped me to heal from my own difficult past, which continued its grip on my present. My family had disintegrated with the death of my mother from leukemia when I was five years old. My father had abandoned my older brother and me to the care of relatives. His mother, an elderly martinet, became my guardian, and I went to live in virtual isolation—except for horses—at her home in Rye, New York and, a few months later, on her estate in South Carolina. My brother and I were separated, as he was sent to a boarding school in another state.

I spent my adult years distancing myself as much as possible from the stranger-relatives among whom I had subsequently been passed, who had taken me in grudgingly. I had severed my relationship with the past, or so I thought. I had believed that I was destined to be alone in this world.

Lay Me Down showed me how wrong I was. Her affectionate spirit, her willingness to risk loving me after all she had been through, was an inspiration. The novels I had labored over were written so I could call myself a writer. The memoir was created in honor of Lay Me Down, as a tribute to her. After I finished it, I thought I understood the magnitude of what she had given me. Then the book, entitled *Chosen by a Horse,* was published in 2006 and I learned that the most profound gifts were still to come.

Not all gifts look appealing at first. When my publisher decided to send me on a regional book tour beginning that spring, I was fearful and shy. Readings, book signings, newspaper and radio interviews—the public face of publishing was exciting but difficult for me, as someone who had lived a relatively solitary life tucked away on a small horse farm for so many years. But the tour was a boon, bringing me back in touch with old friends and important family members with whom I had lost contact. The tour was a reminder that when you're doing what you're supposed to be doing in this life, amazing things can happen.

{ 1 }

HAD COMPLETED A first novel in 1997. Then I'd worked hard on writing a good query letter. I put as much effort into it as I had into writing the manuscript. I kept it really brief: a four-sentence synopsis of the book, a short paragraph about my professional background, and a one-sentence endorsement of the manuscript from a well-known author who had read it.

I'd sent out one hundred of these query letters, all at the same time. Twenty-five agents responded, asking to see the full manuscript and of those, four had offered me representation. All of this had taken more than a year, one long year of facing the weekly rejections. I had dreaded going to the mailbox. Sometime during that year the sleepless nights began, the nights of lying in a fetal position, then turning to stare at the ceiling. My animals kept me going, a pug tucked under one arm, my two Siamese cats under another, and my collie mix stretched across the foot of the bed. If it hadn't been for them and having to get up to feed horses and go to work, I don't know what would have become of me.

I was able to get a wonderful agent at a famous agency. I met the agent, whose reputation overawed me, in her beautiful New York City office, which was decorated like an East Hampton summer cottage with wicker furniture and gleaming hardwood floors. She was surrounded by her authors, their books displayed on three walls, every one of them a renowned literary name. This agent spoke to me as though my novel were already a success, as though I were already one of the elite gracing her walls.

"I expect to get about twenty thousand for this book," she said. "First novels are always the hardest. But for your second we'll get much more and for the third, well . . ." She didn't finish but I was right up there in the clouds with her, floating around in this rosy vision of my literary success.

The rejections from publishers began arriving almost right away. One, two, five, twelve. Thoughtfully, she'd enclose the rejection letter from the publisher along with her own comments about why she thought the novel had failed at that particular house. I forced myself to read these letters, imagining that there was something to be learned but hating to learn it, hating this evidence of my failure. I started a file for rejections and watched it thicken.

After about a year, the rejection letters came less often and then hardly at all and then they stopped. After months of silence, I worked up the nerve to call my agent and left a message that was never returned. More months passed before I left a second message that was never returned and then, one day, she returned the manuscript with a one-line note of apology for being unable to sell it.

The nights got longer and even the days seemed dark. There were glimpses of light but never for long. Two more agents came and went. Nothing changed but their furniture. Years passed. I fell in love with a wonderful man named Paul. My beloved dogs and horses aged and died. I refilled the barn with horse boarders. My brother and sister-in-law gave me a chocolate Lab puppy and I adopted two pug siblings whose owner was leaving the country. During the day I went to my job as a social worker, then to a new job as a writing adjunct at Marist College and a few years after that, to another new job as a writing adjunct at Ulster County Community College. During all those years I got up at 5:00 a.m. every day to work on a second novel, then a third, and finally a memoir about Lay Me Down. I don't know how I kept writing through all the rejections, all the voices telling me I wasn't good enough. I just did. Quitting didn't seem to be an option.

I had liked doing social work and had often felt passionate about it, particularly in the early years. I felt the same way about teaching. Both jobs passed the ultimate question with flying colors: Did I get up in the morning looking forward to work? The answer had always been yes. But writing was different. The dilemma wasn't whether I was a good writer or whether I would ever publish. It was simply this—once I began writing, it was impossible to stop. Sometimes it felt like an addiction. It wasn't hard to get up at 5:00 a.m. It wasn't hard to spend a day trying to get a paragraph right. It wasn't hard to turn into a virtual recluse, even when I felt profoundly lonely. What became hard was doing anything else, anything not related to writing. I thought of having a T-shirt made: *Help! I've fallen and I can't get out of the book.* I fell down the writing hole in 1995 and I still haven't gotten out. The truth is, I don't want to.

Nine years passed. I had been in love, or thought I was, with Paul but we had gone our separate ways after six years together. One day I had envisioned myself at the age of eighty, throwing my suitcase into the back of the car for the weekly two-and-a-half-hour excursion to the city to see Paul. He was never going to leave New York City, and I was never going to leave the country. I was already sick of this drive. Thirty more years of it? For the first time in my life I had the peculiar experience of ending a relationship with someone I still cared about.

By now I was with agent number four. Helen was the first agent who didn't tell me I'd written a best seller, the first who'd eliminated hyperbole from any discussion about my writing. I had been recommended to her by an editor friend. At this point, I felt like a charity case.

"I doubt if we can sell the memoir," she'd told me in our first conversation over the phone. "The market for memoirs is mostly celebrity driven."

A rocky start. I still thought abject flattery was a good thing. I mumbled something about how close my first novel had gotten at Random House, how charmed the editor at someplace else had been. I dragged out my famous author quote on its behalf, the one I'd included in every query letter over the past nine years: "It's the female *Catcher in the Rye,* the best manuscript I've read in twenty years."

Helen seemed unimpressed. Switching the conversation back to the memoir, she said, "It *did* make me cry. That must mean something."

Not exactly wild enthusiasm. Still, she liked my writing enough to send out one of the novels and the memoir. She knew a few editors who, she thought, might be willing to take a look.

A few weeks later I walked into the house, tired from a long day of teaching. I went right to the barn to feed the horses, then inside the house to feed the dogs and cats. At about eight o'clock I checked my phone messages. There was only one and it was from Helen. "Call me as soon as you get this." Her voice was upbeat.

I called and she told me we'd gotten an offer for the memoir. A small offer, an advance of seven thousand dollars, from Soho Press. "I think I can get it up to eight," she said.

I thought about all the years of getting up at five o'clock to write before work, the hundreds of hours that went into writing a book. I thought about the effort it took to persevere. In that light, the offer seemed ridiculous, even insulting. But even as those thoughts ran through my head, I knew money was the wrong thing to focus on. If money was the standard, I'd need a million dollars to make up for what I'd put myself through.

"What do you think?" I asked Helen.

She didn't hesitate. "I think we should take it."

We'd actually gotten a smaller offer a few weeks earlier from an even smaller press. But that offer had fallen apart, nixed by the money people, who were afraid to take on a memoir from an author without a "platform," an author who was a nobody.

Helen explained that an advance was only a down payment against royalties to be earned. I might never earn more but there was a chance I would. So the publisher and I would be partners going forward, and the less money they paid out ahead of time, the more they would be able to invest in promoting the book, which, in the long run, they hoped would be to everyone's benefit.

In the end, selling the book for an eight-thousand-dollar advance felt fine. I had the deep satisfaction of being accepted for publication.

* * *

IN AUGUST 2005, after putting maximum thought and effort into my appearance, I drove into the city for what felt like one of the most important meetings of my life, my first meeting with my publisher. After parking the car, I walked through Union Square to get to Broadway. It was over 100 degrees in the shade. Before I'd crossed the park, I was dizzy from the heat and soaked in sweat. I looked at the people around me, shocked they appeared to be functioning so normally. As I stood on the corner waiting to cross Broadway, a bus roared by, blasting me with diesel fumes and grit. I could feel the grit embedded in my lipstick, glued to my arms and legs with sweat. Every few feet I pulled my black linen dress away from where it clung to my back and thighs. I glanced down at my newly manicured toes, now gray, covered with dust, slipping around in sweaty sandals. I could just imagine what I smelled like. All the planning, all the fantasies about this meeting, this ever-so-important first impression, ruined. It was beyond awful.

My hands were so wet I could barely hold the pen as I signed the guest register in the lobby of the building. Between the heat and my own sky-high anxiety, I was functioning in some kind of altered state. A few minutes later, I walked into the offices of Soho Press for the first time and was greeted by a young woman who smiled and said, "We're so excited to meet you." She offered me a chair at a circular black table in the reception area and went to fetch my editor, Laura. Behind me was a ten-foot-high wall of Soho's books that ran the entire width of the office. In front of me was a bank of tall, grimy windows that looked directly into the windows of the office building across the street. There were several small, open cubicle offices in front of the windows and in each a man or a woman was reading a manuscript. I was surprised to see that someone in a publishing house actually read manuscripts. I had always imagined that some underling glanced at the first few lines of a submission before Frisbeeing it onto the heap of other manuscripts piled in a corner. I got up and walked over to one of the young women.

"Do you get many good ones?" I asked.

"Not as good as yours," she said.

I didn't know which shocked me more, what she said or that she knew who I was. I thanked her and returned to my chair to wait for Laura. A thought ran through my head on a continuous loop. *I am in my publisher's office.* The walls were painted a dull gray, matched by worn gray carpeting. I sat at a table they must have used for conferences. The rest of the desks and chairs I could see were a forgettable miscellany of standard office furniture. Whatever air-conditioning existed wasn't working and the office was hot. Not exactly the mahogany-paneled sanctuary I had imagined a publisher's office would be. But I was dazzled anyway, to have entered this most elusive of clubs.

Laura appeared, a woman of average height with a trim figure and graying brown hair. She wore a black polo shirt and gray slacks.

I stood up to shake her hand.

"Oh dear," she said and immediately left to get me a glass of water.

I wondered what had alarmed her: my still wet hand, the damp hair plastered to my head, the little pieces of grit adorning my red lipstick, or my dress clinging to me like a bath towel?

She returned with ice water and we sat down right there at the round black table. I was finally face to face with the woman who, in editing my manuscript, had noted in the margin next to a sentence marked for deletion, *Dreadful.*

"We're very excited about this book," she said.

Had she forgiven me for *dreadful?* "I'm excited, too," I told her and handed her a straw beach tote filled with little gifts as a thank you to her for buying my book, for giving me this incredible moment. I had been uncertain about giving her anything, about what the protocol was for thanking a publisher for publishing me. I had no idea what other authors did but in the end I didn't care. I did what was in my heart and had had fun choosing the gifts for this woman I hadn't yet met.

She seemed surprised and put the tote on the floor next to her with no sign that she intended to open any of the brightly wrapped gifts spilling out of the open top. Later, I received a lovely thank-you note from her.

"Our publicity director should be here any minute," she said, "and then we'll go to lunch."

Kathy, the publicist, arrived, and I was struck by her youth and prettiness. She was short, even shorter than I am, with curly, shoulder-length black hair and a radiant smile. The three of us walked the few blocks to the Blue Water Grill in Union Square. I felt sickened by the sun whenever we left the shade of a building. The air-conditioning in the restaurant was doing its job, though, and for the first time since arriving in New York that day, I began to cool down and relax.

Both Laura and I focused on Kathy. She had a sparkly intelligence and a wonderful magnetic wit. Originally from the Midwest, she had recently moved to New York to work

for Soho after a stint with a publisher in Boston. She had
come to New York without knowing a soul, something I
never would have had the courage to do. I don't remember
much of what we talked about but it was during that lunch
that the idea of a book tour was first discussed.

Over the hour-and-a-half lunch, I liked them both more
and more. Originally, I had felt a little disappointed that
the book had sold to a small press. Part of me had wanted
the glamour of a big house, the cachet. A big house meant a
"big" book, more prestige. More something. But over lunch
that feeling vanished. I had stumbled into the perfect publishing house. Over the next few months, that feeling grew.
Working on the book with my editor, Laura, and then my
copy editor, Pat, proved to be a joy. After all those years of
laboring alone, it was good to collaborate with others. For
the first time I felt that my work was being honored. It
would have been perfectly OK if my getting-published story
had ended there. But it didn't. It had just begun.

SIX MONTHS LATER, on a dreary day in late February,
three months before the scheduled publication date of my
book, June first, I came home early from work to another
message from Helen. "Call Laura first and then call me."
There was that upbeat tone in her voice again, the one that
meant good news.

I called Laura at Soho. I'll never forget her voice. She
sounded calm and matter-of-fact. "Harcourt Brace pur-
chased the paperback rights to your book today for a hundred thousand dollars," she said.

I think I said, *What?* I was standing in the kitchen and I
started to walk around in little circles with the phone

jammed against my ear. My knees wobbled and my hands shook. I started to cry.

Laura described the sale in detail, how she was afraid she'd lost the deal entirely when she'd refused an offer of seventy-five thousand on a Friday afternoon. "Over the weekend I thought, Oh dear, maybe I've lost Susan a lot of money." But on Monday morning they had come back with a bigger offer. She told me all of this in her flat, calm voice, explaining that I would receive about half of this sum, as the purchase price would be split between publisher and author. I couldn't take it all in. That my work—turned down by so many—had been deemed worthy of this amount of money! I kept interrupting her to say, *Thank you, Laura, thank you*.

It was a brief conversation, less than five minutes, and when we hung up I sat on a stool at the kitchen counter and wept, completely overwhelmed. A few minutes later I picked up the phone and called my brother.

We are both writers but he's older, smarter, more determined. He's a lawyer by day and a writer in whatever stolen moments he can grab—5:00 a.m., nights, weekends. In the natural order of things, this should have been Lloyd's triumph. He has written two books; for a while he was represented by one of the biggest agencies in New York City. We'd shared our getting-dumped-by-agent stories. I was ahead of him by three on that score but he'd been dumped from a greater height, which sort of equalized things.

For ten years we'd been e-mailing each other about our authorial travails, sometimes in painful detail. For Christmas a few years ago, he had presented me with two huge notebooks filled with a complete record of our e-mails to each other covering a six-year period. You had to be crazy or a writer to care about such a thing. I treasured them. Writing isn't for people with thin skins and we both had thin skins, at least for the first few years. I don't know how we'd survived all the bad news except that we'd shared it with each other. Sometimes we could joke about it but most of the time it seemed to cripple us in spirit. It was impossible not to consider the complexity of how he might feel about success hitting so close to home. I knew he would be happy for me, I knew he would be proud. I'll never forget the phone call I got from him the first time he read *Chosen by a Horse*.

It was Thanksgiving, six months before the book came out. I had sent him a bound galley and a note of thanks, telling him how much his support had meant to me, how much I cherished him as a brother. I was spending the holiday in Maine with two friends at a house on the ocean we had rented for the week. I hadn't bothered to give anyone the land-line number because I assumed we'd be using our cell phones. But it turned out there was no cell-phone reception so after my brother read my book, he couldn't reach me. It took a lot of ingenuity on his part to track me down. One night I was surprised to hear his voice on the telephone.

"*Why don't you ever leave a number?*" He was exasperated.

"Sorry," I said.

Then he burst into tears. I don't mean his voice quivered; I mean he *burst* into tears. He could hardly talk he was crying so hard.

"It's *towering*," he sobbed, "a *towering* work."

Towering? My slim, quiet book was towering? I was paralyzed. My brother didn't just like my book, it seemed to have broken his heart, or rather, entered his heart. It was as though until that moment, he hadn't really known who I was, what his little sister was all about. I don't think he quite believed I was a writer. And why should he have? All he'd ever seen were copies of rejection letters and years of e-mails from me saying things like, *My writing sucks, I'm too dumb to write, I don't know what I'm doing.* And then I'd sent him a galley of a book about horses, a subject about which my brother has no interest. Zero. Frankly, I was surprised he'd read it.

When I had first begun the project, when I first told him I was writing a memoir about one of my horses, he had seemed skeptical, even dismissive. It was not a subject he thought would exactly rocket me into publishing.

"I started a new book today," I had told him over the phone, "about when I adopted Lay Me Down."

After a longish silence (my brother is rareley at a loss for words), he had cleared his throat and said, "Have you given any thought to getting a full-time job, Sooz?"

Pretty much everyone I mentioned it to felt that way.

And, yes, I had considered working full-time, if you counted sitting bolt upright in bed in the middle of an anxiety attack at 2:00 a.m., wondering how to make the two thousand dollars in my checking account cover the four thousand dollars' worth of bills sitting on my desk. In fact, I'd even gone on a job search if you counted ordering the book about beekeeping from Amazon.com when I was contemplating going into the honey-selling business.

"Honeycombs weigh eighty pounds," a neighbor had pointed out. "How are you going to lift eighty pounds with your bad back?"

The bee book hadn't mentioned that.

"I feel a lot of energy around this subject," I'd explained to my brother. It had sounded flaky even to me, but it was true. I wanted to write about my horse Lay Me Down and how, because of her, one morning on my way to work, in the middle of the Rhinecliff Bridge, I'd seen who I was clearly for the first time in my life. I don't think we get those moments too often, moments of such clarity they change your life right on the spot.

I HAD BEEN a social worker then, on my way to work in a private residential treatment facility. I was on my way to help others who, for one reason or another, were not able to help themselves. I was the one who sat behind the big desk with a pen in my hand, taking notes about the person on the other side of the desk who had all the problems.

Three things had me on edge that December morning. It was my forty-fifth birthday; it was almost Christmas day, the day I had last seen my mother alive; and I had a dying horse I loved whom I was taking to Cornell the next day for one last attempt to save her life. I must have been thinking about death, about my own, my mother's, possibly my horse's, when in the middle of the Rhinecliff Bridge, I *saw inside my body*. It was spooky enough to suddenly have my midsection become like the glass wall of an aquarium that lets you see things in the ocean that would never have been possible to see before. And maybe if what I had seen was something as pretty as a coral reef or as brilliant as a neon tetra it would have been strange but OK. But that's not what I saw as clearly as you see the words on this page. Instead it was a mountain of burning fire, and it took up the whole inside of me from my chest to my hips. The image only lasted a second but in that second I learned who I was; I learned the *truth* about me. I was a person who was consumed with anger and sorrow. I was *raging.* There it was, as clear as a CNN headline, *Woman on Fire.* I understood that the fire had been there a long time, at least forty years, since the death of my mother. I understood that it was the driving force in my life, that it required most of my energy to work around it, to ignore it, to not know it was there. I knew that it was killing me. I was surprised it hadn't finished me off already. I understood how living with rage can eat away at you, can kill you cell by cell, keep you more dead than alive because to be fully alive would mean *feeling the pain of that fire and I was too afraid to do that.*

I knew all this in less than a second on the bridge. The sweet, helpful woman who had woken up that morning to drive to work was gone, vanished. She had never really existed. She was someone I must have made up, read about in a book, some child's story about a nice little girl who helps others less fortunate, who smiles a lot. She was someone, *anyone,* other than who she really was: helpless, enraged, grief-stricken.

I was terrified. It wasn't what I thought would happen to me driving to work that day. It wasn't what I thought would happen to me ever, that kind of hallucinatory insight. I had never taken drugs during the sixties precisely because I had no desire for such mind-blowing visions. I had no desire to alter my consciousness and no wonder—God knows what else I might have seen.

It was months before I recovered from that experience on the bridge. I was afraid it might happen again, that suddenly I was going to become a person who hallucinated on a regular basis, that I had quietly gone around the bend and wouldn't be coming back. But the other question that haunted me was *What was I going to do about it?* The anger, the rage, the sorrow? The burning mountain? Now that I could no longer pretend I didn't know it was there, that it was at the very core of me, how did I put it out? *Could* I put it out? It took years to learn the answer to that question.

THOSE FEW MOMENTS on the phone listening to my brother cry, listening to him tell me what he liked about the book subtly changed our relationship. I was no longer just the little sister, the annoying entity who had come along and sucked up his oxygen when he was eighteen months old, forcing him to share the spotlight, a role I suspect many first children don't cherish. Suddenly, with this book, I had become an equal. There was a new respect in his voice. There was pride.

But there must have also been jealousy, envy, something less magnanimous. Not that he ever showed it, but it must have been there because he is human. We had been working hard toward the same goal and the one who reached it first wasn't necessarily the one who deserved it more. So much of publishing is luck; the right editor reading the right manuscript at the right moment. Still, hearing the admiration in my brother's voice was deeply gratifying, an unexpected gift of publishing.

NOW, AS I told him shakily about the news of the paperback sale I had just been given, "Don't count your chickens before they hatch," he said.

He'd misunderstood. "No," I told him, "it's a done deal."

It took him a few seconds but it finally sank in. "God, Sooz, that's *terrific,*" my brother said.

T WAS THE SPRING of 2006. Soho had meant what they'd said about promoting my book. Not only had it been sent far and wide in handsome prepublication promotional galleys, they had organized a regional book tour for me. Part of all the planned readings, the one I'd been looking forward to the longest, yet with the deepest dread, was one I was responsible for, my first scheduled reading, at the Golden Notebook in Woodstock, New York. It was a small store with books crammed floor to ceiling and many more stacked in teetering piles in corners. It was a book lover's bookstore in a town famous for its writers, artists, and musicians. I'd made the mistake of telling Barry, the owner, way too early that I was trying to publish a novel. For the next seven years, whenever I walked into the store Barry would say, "How's it going? Any luck?"

When he first started asking, say the first year or two, I'd smile back, pleased that he'd remembered to ask, and shake my head, no, no luck. "Well," he'd say, this man wise in the ways of the nefarious book-publishing world, "it's too soon to get discouraged."

At some point after year two, "It's too soon to get discouraged" became "I know a guy whose book was rejected for five years straight"—eight years, ten years, fill in the blank—and "Look," he'd say, pointing to a spot on the floor where the newly published book had assumed an honored place in a tilting three-foot tower, "look what happens if you stick it out."

I desperately wanted my book to end up in a tower on the floor of Barry's store. What an achievement. What a thrill. I made a point of imagining it there. Visualization. An important part of achieving any goal. Over the years, going into Barry's store became harder. But I was an inveterate book buyer and I wanted to support my locally owned, independent bookseller. I had no choice. It was the Golden Notebook or nothing.

Three years passed, four years, five, six, *seven*. I could hardly look Barry in the eyes. I hated that I'd ever told him I was writing. I hated my failure. I tried to sneak into the store. It was difficult with the checkout counter right next to the front door. Just when I thought I was safe, "Any luck?" would drift over the stack I was hiding behind.

One day, seven years later, I walked into the store and got to say this: "BARRY, I SOLD A BOOK!"

And after congratulating me, Barry got to say this back: "I'll set up a reading for you here."

My heart sank. A reading in Woodstock? A town jam-packed with, well, *real* talent. *Real* writers.

"It's just a memoir," I apologized. Not a novel. Not quite a real book.

"Terrific," he said. "I'll schedule the reading right around your publication date. How's mid-May?"

Wasn't this exactly what I wanted? Publication and whatever came with it? The title of my book peeking out of the pile on Barry's floor? A spot on a library shelf? Readings? Recognition from the literary community I had felt shut out of for seven years?

Yes, I wanted all of that. But suddenly I had a new set of worries.

I had stood in front of large groups of students to teach writing for eight years and rarely felt the slightest bit nervous. But this would be different. For the first time, I would be the focus of the group, not the work of another writer or student—*me*. I had never before in my life been the center of attention. For years I had fantasized about what this would be like, one of my many fantasies about what it would be like to get published. I'd always imagined that it would be easy, even pleasant. Now the thought of reading from my book filled me with anxiety. And I had agreed to a whole summer of it.

For seven years I'd been focused on agents and publishers. Writing a book had meant first interesting an agent enough to represent it, and then interesting a publisher enough to buy it. I had so feared I'd never get past the gatekeepers of the industry—between agents and publishers probably no more than several hundred men and women—that I had never thought past that point. It had just dawned on me that in writing a memoir I had basically invited the whole world to examine my life with a magnifying glass. *What had I been thinking?*

I felt a hot flash building. It started in the center of my chest and radiated in every direction until my temples throbbed and I was covered in a fine sweat. I hadn't considered how exposed I might feel. How ashamed at what strangers would know about me. I was horrified. I wanted to call Soho and stop publication. I wanted to give the money back. I was flooded with contradictory fears: *no one* would buy the book, and I would die of shame; *everyone* would buy the book, and I would die of shame.

Now the chances for rejection had become *limitless*. This new round of rejections would come from readers, beginning with no one showing up for my reading at the Golden Notebook. This was the real world. *Why on earth had I wanted this?*

NOBODY SHOWING UP was an old fear based on harsh experience. In my childhood, nobody *had* come. "Nobody" mostly meant my father and brother. They were the only two relatives still alive I could claim as my own. They never came to anything—not to birthdays, not to graduations, not to Christmas.

For years I had no idea where my father was. I knew where my brother was, but we didn't live together and I was too young to do anything about it. So was he.

After my mother's death, I'd lived with a series of relatives who resented the responsibility of raising me. I knew this deeply and profoundly. To survive their anger at my presence—sometimes their physical attacks—I tried to remain invisible. I stayed in my room. I ingratiated myself. I asked for nothing. I smiled. I was that dog groveling on its belly in front of someone with a stick. It sickens me to think of it.

When I was nine, living with an aunt and uncle outside of Boston, I had been told that my father was coming to visit me after an absence of four years. As soon as breakfast was over, I dragged a child-sized rocking chair to the end of the driveway and waited for the strange car that would be his. I was like a bird dog on point, my posture rigid, my eyes fixed on the spot on the road where his car would first be visible. I couldn't leave my post, not even hours later when I had to go to the bathroom. Even I knew this behavior was a little strange. By dinnertime, my aunt and uncle forced me to abandon that post. "He's not coming," my aunt said. I couldn't look at her. I couldn't look at anyone. The shame was breathtaking.

A few years later, I was attending the Northampton School for Girls, a prep school in Western Massachusetts my grandmother had sent me to after I begged her to stop making me live with any more relatives. I was thirteen and it was my first year there. My grandmother had written to tell me that my father would be coming for Parents' Day. I still hadn't seen him or heard from him since I was five. My roommate's parents called and wrote to her several times a week. I tried to imagine having such a parent. How would I feel? Would I dislike the hovering, the constant attention? No, I decided, every time she got a call or a letter. I would soak it up and bask in it, and I would never ever take it for granted.

The morning of Parents' Day I waited at the window for the strange car that would be his to park in front of the dorm. I waited all day long until my roommate's parents suggested I join them for dinner at the fancy hotel in town. I went, I ate, I smiled. They were kind but I was wretched, and on top of it all I felt guilty because I was sure I'd spoiled their dinner, sure that they had really wanted to spend time alone with their daughter.

I carried this baggage into adulthood. I assumed no one would show up, so I didn't invite anyone to anything important. Not to my college graduation, graduate school graduation, my wedding, birthdays, holidays, nothing. Not because I didn't want to invite people. I did. But what if I did and no one showed up once again? The possibility of another disappointment was too big for me to face.

NOBODY WOULD COME to my reading at the Golden Notebook. Of this I was sure. Kathy at Soho had been setting up readings all over New England. I'd been helping her by suggesting bookstores in towns where I knew people. Even as I did this, I couldn't shake my dread that no one would come. It loomed over me. I developed acid indigestion. At first it was once or twice a week. Soon I was taking Prilosec daily. My stomach was a hard knot tucked high under my diaphragm. The Golden Notebook reading was scheduled to take place before the book was officially published. Before anyone had a chance to read it. Why would anyone come?

MAY 20 ARRIVED, the day of my reading at the Golden Notebook. *Chosen by a Horse* had been in stores for about a week. It had gotten a few good early "trade" reviews: from *Kirkus Reviews, Publishers Weekly,* and *Library Journal.* I was too new to publishing to appreciate how special a good book review was, to be grateful that my book had been reviewed at all. I don't know how I'd come so far understanding so little about the book-publishing process. I knew one side of it pretty well, the outside. But everything that happened after the day Soho bought my book was new and *news* to me.

"Have you checked your Amazon.com ranking?" someone asked.

"What's that?" I said.

"Do you know your ISBN number?'"

"I have no idea." I knew that every book published is assigned an ISBN—International Standard Book Number.

I'd been phoning, e-mailing, and sending out postcards to everyone I knew for weeks, asking them, begging them, *bribing* them to come to my reading. It seemed like a lot of them were going to be out of town, at school functions for their children, at events and activities far away from Woodstock, New York. I rubbed the knot where my stomach used to be. I practiced what I would say to Barry when he found out he was stuck with forty-five autographed books.

As if my anxiety wasn't sky-high enough, I'd also decided to host a party at my house following the reading. It meant planning, cooking, cleaning, arranging. To be fair, friends had offered to do this, to host a publication party for me. But I'd declined. I had to have this party at my house because this was where my four horses, including Lay Me Down, were buried. None of this would be happening if it hadn't been for Lay Me Down. I kept her photograph Scotch-taped to the side of my computer, as close to me as I could get it to keep her inspiration fresh. Her eyes were a constant reminder of all the ways she had enriched my life. This party was for her, in full view of her grave in the back pasture just beyond the pond. In full view of the graves of all four of them: Lay Me Down, Georgia, Hotshot, and Tempo. They were all in the book and now they were dead. I wanted to honor them, to include them, to have them near me at this moment. But Lay Me Down, *especially* Lay Me Down, I wanted to be celebrated.

I didn't know how many people would come, so I planned food for about thirty. My house wasn't big enough for so many unless we stood nose to nose or like people riding in an elevator. It was a thousand-square-foot house of post-and-beam design, made to look like a converted barn. The living room, dining room, and kitchen were one open area with glass walls going up to a cathedral ceiling. A spiral staircase led to the master bedroom and bath. Off the downstairs hallway was another bathroom, a guest room, and my office. It was exactly the same as it had been on the day I'd bought it except for a fresh coat of paint and the six-stall horse barn I'd had built in the field next to the house. In spite of its small size, because of its rough, barnlike design, and open views to the pond, meadows, and mountains, I thought it was the most wonderful house I'd ever lived in. For the party, I'd planned to open both sets of sliding glass doors off the living/dining room to the deck and set up additional tables and chairs there. It would have been the perfect solution for a warm spring night, but on this May 20 the temperature was in the high forties. No one would want to go outside.

I couldn't bear to think about this so I began to obsess about something else instead: what to wear. I stood at my open closet door and considered the possibilities: the baggy black Tencel pants with a baggy black shirt or the baggy khaki Tencel pants with a baggy black shirt? I could throw a baggy maroon vest over either and *Voila!* I would be tented, completely protected, which was exactly how I wanted to be. I went for the all-black look and while I was standing in front of the bathroom mirror applying mascara and blush, I thought, Why would anyone come to hear a fat old woman read from a book about a dying horse on a Saturday night in Woodstock when there are so many more amusing things to do?

I fled from the image in the mirror as a hot flash built and by the time I was in the kitchen checking the platters of food spread out on the kitchen counter, it felt like I'd taken a shower and put clothes on before toweling off. I briefly considered changing but vanity won; it was better to be damp in black than lumpy in khaki.

I don't remember how I got to Woodstock. It is seventeen miles from my house so it must have been by car, and I probably rode with someone else, but it's a complete blank. The first thing I do remember is standing under a sycamore tree in front of Joshua's Restaurant, where the reading would take place in an upstairs area. I was with a group of friends but the only one I remember clearly is Elaine, whose presence has a calming effect on me. I ate dinner at her house so often that I had my own dinner tray stacked on top of the refrigerator along with hers and her husband's. We'd carry our trays of food upstairs and eat while watching *Jeopardy*. Her husband, Francis, was good at the history and science questions, I was pretty good at literature and politics, and Elaine was good at philosophy and religion. Still, even with our combined "expertise," we seemed to get most of the answers wrong.

People I knew were beginning to arrive for the reading. They stopped under the sycamore tree to say hello first before going into Joshua's and heading up the stairs. I was so anxious I forgot the names of people I'd known for twenty years. Because of this, I could not introduce anyone to anyone else. I seemed to be in a permanent hot flash.

"This is *awful*," I whispered to Elaine. Not that people were coming or that I didn't know their names, but that I was so consumed by anxiety I was incapable of thinking clearly. It was impossible to enjoy this moment.

"Just relax," said Elaine.

What? How?

"Shouldn't you go in?" she asked.

It was five minutes to five. I nodded and we went in and climbed the narrow stairs to the small banquet room on the second floor. I'd eaten at Joshua's often over the past twenty-four years, but I'd never been upstairs. I was surprised to see that it was filled with natural light from the two walls of windows that overlooked the street. There was a small bar along a windowless wall and the rest of the room was occupied by an assortment of chairs, tables, and couches. It was homey and intimate. Barry had set up a table in the back of the room stacked with books. He smiled and waved when he saw me.

"Where should I sit?" I asked him.

I made my way to the table he indicated, clutching a bound galley of the book, saying hello to people as I went. I was amazed that I had risked inviting people to something as important to me as this reading, and I was amazed they had come. If I thought about it, I would cry. No one in the room had any idea what an enormous thing was happening. Forget about publishing, forget about reading in a town full of better writers, what was incredible was that there was a room full of people here *for me.*

I knew most of the thirty or so people there, but a few were strangers to me. One was a pretty auburn-haired woman sitting alone at a table in the window. I walked over to introduce myself, to thank her for coming. Her name was Lee Harrington and she, too, had just published a book, a memoir about how she and her husband had met and married because of a rescue dog. I made a mental note to buy a copy of the book. I liked the title, *Rex and the City,* and wished mine was that clever. We spoke for a minute, comparing publishing experiences. She was with a big house that was doing virtually no marketing for her memoir. I was with a small house that was doing a lot. We noted the irony of this. I was surprised and flattered that an author had come to my reading. I thought of her as a *real* writer. I saw that she had brought a stack of postcards promoting her book. I took one so I could hold it up and tell the group about it. It was the first time I'd been in the position to help another writer, in even a small way, and I relished it.

Finally, I sat on the stool in front of the room. It felt like I'd reached the end of a pilgrimage, an epic journey that had begun when I was five and started to learn that I would spend the rest of my life trying to find my place, trying to find my people. I'd made many mistakes along the way, often increasing my feelings of alienation by choosing the wrong places and the wrong people. But as I looked around this sunny room at Joshua's, filled with friends, some of my students, and a few strangers who shared a love of books, I thought that I had found what I had been seeking.

"Publishing a book won't fix your life," a published friend had cautioned me once as I sat on the couch in his living room with the latest rejection letter in my hand. I was overwhelmed by despair. "The truth is, publishing doesn't change anything," he'd said.

I didn't believe him. His own book, a memoir about growing up in Newfoundland before moving to New York City and becoming a theater critic, peeked out at us from a bookshelf right behind him. It was a good book, beautifully crafted, smart. Of course it had changed his life. It had even changed mine. Good stories can do that, connect us to each other and make us feel less alone. Books are profound in that way. They are survival kits. Open them up and inside is a set of instructions for how to live, for how to be human, for how to love.

Now I knew he had been wrong. Publishing a book had given me this moment at Joshua's, this extraordinary feeling of being part of a community. It had taken me fifty years to drag that rocking chair to the end of the driveway again, to wait for a sign that I belonged to someone. And now, with the publication of this book, at this first public reading to celebrate its existence, I had found it. Because this time my family had come.

{ 3 }

*M*Y SECOND READING was scheduled for the following day. That Sunday dawned windy and cold and then it rained on and off all day. I was tired from the publication party I'd given at my house the night before, tired from getting up at six to do a radio interview at WDST in Woodstock earlier that morning, tired of feeling anxious and crazy about what was confronting me. The most wonderful thing had happened and I couldn't relax and enjoy it for more than a few minutes here and there when I was able to forget that I was facing a book tour.

I had just parked my car in the lot of the Catskill Animal Sanctuary, where I was scheduled to read at a fund-raiser.

"Congratulations on the book," someone said as she passed me.

"Thank you." I smiled, finding it difficult to look her in the eye, to fully absorb the compliment. Being acknowledged and accepting attention was an effort. I was so used to hiding. I'd done it all my life. But publishing a book had made that impossible.

Surrounded by two hundred acres and populated by rescued farm animals, the sanctuary had seemed to me the perfect place to read from a book about a rescued horse. I was looking forward to meeting their latest addition, Franklin, a five-week-old pig. He was featured on the flier announcing the event, a tiny pink pig with pink eyelashes walking on tip-toes through lush green grass. I had imagined myself reading from my book while cradling Franklin in my free arm, a grown-up Fern from *Charlotte's Web* with her baby pig. In fact, I had imagined reading in the large barn that is the setting of *Charlotte's Web,* with the heads of horses, sheep, goats, and pigs bobbing over stall doors, while people sat around on bales of hay and upturned buckets scattered along the center aisle. I mentioned this to the owner and director of the sanctuary, who said that too many people in the barn at one time might distress some of the animals, who were still recovering from abuse and neglect. I liked that she considered them first. Still, I was disappointed.

I'd arrived early so I could spend time visiting the animals and have a turn to hold Franklin. My friend Dorothy had driven with me and two other friends, Elaine and Francis, had followed us in their car. No one was visible when we arrived except a man and a woman taking down a food tent. It was four o'clock and many people with small children had already left for the day. The more adult activities would begin at five: a live jazz band, a wine tasting hosted by a local vineyard, and my reading. I was not exactly sure in what order.

The weather worsened. As soon as we got out of the car, Dorothy and I bowed our heads into a cold wind and zipped up our coats. Around us the ground was wet and muddy. Dorothy was wearing khaki capris, open-toed mules, and a light spring jacket. I didn't know what she had been expecting, but she always dresses better than I do, no matter where we go. At least I had on heavy Solomon snow shoes, my crummiest black corduroy pants, and an old red parka.

Perfect for walking through manure and getting peed on by baby pigs.

Across the parking lot in a tent I spotted Gretchen, a colleague at the community college where I teach. She was on the sanctuary's board of directors, and was responsible for inviting me to read. We waved to one another as I walked toward the table where she was trying to reorganize the stacks of information and brochures about the sanctuary and animal rescue efforts that had been blown around by the wind. I bent to help her look for rocks heavy enough to use as paperweights.

"This is totally horrible," she said, disgusted by the weather because it would affect turnout and the sanctuary would raise less money. Passionate about animal welfare, Gretchen volunteers hours of her time for the cause.

"It'll be OK," I said because I hated to see her upset. I knew how hard she had worked helping to organize this day. She'd been talking about it for weeks at the Ulster County Community College writing center where we tutored together.

"It sucks," she said, refusing to be placated. Behind us in another tent, the band—four or five young men—were setting up. None of them looked over twenty. Gretchen followed my glance. "If that's a jazz band I'm the Pope," she said.

The wind picked up, and it started to rain hard. The sides of the tent snapped at their rope moorings and the rocks we'd placed on the table rolled off, freeing brochures to fly across the parking lot. Gretchen and I ran after them, fishing them out of muddy puddles.

"Where's Franklin?" I asked, desperate to raise our spirits.

She perked up instantly. "In the barn," she said, in the squeaky voice of a baby pig. "Wanna meet him?"

We were standing on a small hill on one side of the parking lot, clutching a bunch of muddy brochures. Below us was the tent where the brochures should have been, and behind that was another tent where the probably-not-a-jazz-band was setting up. In the near distance was a long, low building where farm equipment was stored and past that was the main barn where many of the animals were housed. Stretching into the distance as far as the eye could see were large pastures with turnout sheds for horses and cows. This two-hundred-acre valley nestled between wooded ridges on either side really felt like a sanctuary, a place an animal could finally come to be safe.

We watched a man and a woman get out of a car in the parking lot below us. The man had a trimmed gray mustache and goatee and was wearing a yellow raincoat and a khaki-colored baseball cap. The woman had soft blonde hair swept into a bun and was wearing jeans and knee-high green muck-out boots. They were a handsome couple. For some reason, I was mesmerized by them.

The rain shower ended as Gretchen and I walked back to the tent to straighten out the brochure table again, replacing the rocks with bigger ones. Then she went off to finalize details about the evening's events and I collected Dorothy, Elaine, and Francis and we went to find Franklin, the baby pig.

We walked down the center aisle of the dimly lit barn, petting noses and reading the history of each animal, which had been posted next to each stall door. A male goat with large curling horns wandered around free, as did a pot-bellied pig with tiny recessed eyes. We passed a stall where three huge hogs were lying almost on top of each other for warmth, so overweight they could hardly walk. Since coming to the sanctuary they had been put on a healthier diet and were slowly losing weight. Their crippling size typified what the meat industry does to hogs.

We passed a completely blind horse who greeted us with a nicker and leaned hard into any hand that would scratch his neck. We passed stalls of chickens and pygmy goats and finally came to one in which there was a doghouse stuffed with quilts and blankets. This had to be where Franklin was kept. I stepped over the knee-high barrier in front of the doghouse and bent to peek inside. I couldn't see anything in the pile of blankets so I put my hand in to feel around. Right away it bumped into something warm and firm that squealed softly.

The staff at the sanctuary had been taking turns carrying Franklin around and bottle-feeding him, the kind of attention a five-pound baby pig—he was the runt of the litter, left to die by the farmer who owned him—required. I had gotten permission from the staff to take him out and hold him because he would be awakened anyway for a bottle feeding at five.

He squealed plaintively as I pulled him from his bed, but settled quickly and happily inside the warmth of my parka, which I'd zipped over him so just his head stuck out to rest against my shoulder. He was absurdly, shockingly pink. He smelled sweet and slightly milky from his last bottle. He sucked at my thumb making little grunting noises. I would have liked to hold him longer but he had a crowd of admirers waiting their turn. I relinquished him to Elaine, who tucked him inside her own coat, marveling at the translucent pink eyelashes and the tiny tiptoe hooves.

Out of the corner of my eye I became aware of the man

in the yellow raincoat and his pretty blonde wife. They had entered the barn and were wandering down the center aisle, looking over stall doors, bending to pet whatever walked by. I had created a complete fantasy about them, about who they were and what their lives were like. They were bright, interesting people who had been married a long time. Their house was modern and sunny, full of good books and good art. They had traveled a lot and were comfortable anywhere in the world. They were comfortable with each other. I didn't know what they did for a living but whatever it was, it was right and good. They were full of integrity.

I was aware of a gnawing envy and at first I wasn't sure what it was about. Her attractiveness? Her good fortune in having such a handsome husband? Their long, happy marriage? The love they had found? Yes, all of that and more. I envied their confidence, their assuredness. They seemed almost perfect to me, or as close to it as anyone could get.

We spent an hour in the barn visiting the animals, taking turns holding Franklin. A dozen or so others arrived and the barn was filled with the soft murmuring of voices. At five I left to look for Gretchen. I found her once more on the hill above the parking lot, standing with her arms folded, looking disgusted. The probably-not-a-jazz-band had started to play and within minutes it was clear they were definitely-not-a-jazz-band. Loud, discordant rock blasted from their tent, and we watched as several people emerged from their cars and immediately covered their ears.

"This is outrageous," Gretchen said. She had already had a heated discussion with the board member who'd hired the band. She was angry because it was not a jazz band as promised and because they were getting paid too much money,

money that should have gone to the sanctuary. It was also obvious that they were really bad. They sounded like a high-school garage band at their first jam session. We listened for a few more minutes, horrified. The board member who had hired them had told them they could play for the next hour, which meant that I wouldn't be reading until at least six o'clock. Worse, it meant that everyone had to listen to this terrible music for another hour. As if the weather weren't bad enough.

As we stood there, a car arrived and we watched three people get out and pause, listening to the music. Then we watched them get back in the car and drive away. Gretchen was almost in tears.

Just then, the man in the yellow raincoat and his wife appeared, walking toward the parking lot. As they passed the music tent they covered their ears and smiled at each other. It was such an ordinary gesture, a smile exchanged between two people about something—this horrible band—but it added to their appeal, to my fantasy about their closeness. As they walked toward the cars, I was afraid they would leave, that they would get in their car and I'd never see them again. This made me inexplicably sad.

"See that man," I said to Gretchen, pointing discreetly. "If I ever dated again, I would want him to look just like that."

"Oh my God," she said, "I can introduce you. He's totally available."

I was so surprised by her response that I didn't really understand what she meant.

"*She's* just a friend," Gretchen said about the woman who was with him. "They've known each other for years. He's *available*."

Suddenly, he lost all his charm. Even she became less interesting. They were not the poster couple for wedded bliss, exemplars of lifelong intimacy. My whole daydream— the pretty house with all the glass, the trips to Europe, the socially responsible jobs—dissolved, along with their enormous appeal.

"I meant in theory," I said to Gretchen. I've said this to Gretchen many times. "You know I'm done with men." And I meant it. I was done. The only thing I'd failed at more times than trying to find a publisher was trying to find a partner. My record was appalling. I had accepted that I would spend the rest of my life alone. Once that thought had terrified me, but now it was OK. I'd gotten used to it.

Gretchen shook her head at my stubbornness. "He'd be perfect for you."

"Shut up," I said, jabbing her with my elbow. "Help me get my books out of the car."

The now uninteresting man in the yellow raincoat and his companion got into their car and turned on the engine, but they didn't go anywhere. They were not leaving, they were just getting warm.

But who cared?

I set my books up on the damp table under the flapping tent and wondered who would be around to buy any. The terrible noise from the music tent had driven everyone as far from it as they could get. There couldn't have been more than a dozen people in the barn. I saw a few more standing near the fence looking at cows and another car or two had arrived while I was arranging books. I needed to ask the sanctuary's director where I would read. There were chairs set up in the tent, but it was too cold there. Gretchen had

envisioned a large turnout, many dozens of cheerful atten-
dees eager to spend a beautiful spring day and evening enjoying good food, good music, and good wine for a good cause.
Usually the sanctuary attracted just such a crowd at their
fund-raisers. But this time the weather had prevailed.

By 6:30 people were angry and exhausted. The only reason they were still there was because of their devotion to
animals and the sanctuary. Several people had bought my
book and apologized for not staying for the reading. It was
too late, they explained, tomorrow was a workday and they
had to get home. They were shivering as they apologized. I
was, too. I still had no idea where I was to read or even if the
reading was going to happen.

The director appeared and, with the help of several men,
started dragging folding chairs out of the tent and into a small
shed behind it. The band had stopped playing, and it was
mercifully quiet. I was mortified by the dismal turnout, the
dismal music, the dismal weather. I was mortified that I was
apparently expected to read to this handful of freezing, faith-
ful stragglers who desperately wanted to go home but out of
a sense of obligation had remained. It was a nightmare.

The director started herding people into the shed. "It's
warm inside," she told them brightly. "Come in, come in."

We did as we were told. Inside there were about twenty-
five chairs set up in four crescent-shaped rows. At the front
of the shed was a chair for me. I sat, and to my surprise,
watched the seats fill up. Two men came in and sat near the
front, Malcolm and James, old friends of mine from New
York City. They had been on their way back to the city from
their country house when they'd seen the poster advertising
my reading on the wall of a gas station. I was thrilled and

touched that they had come, that they had taken this detour to hear me read. Out of the corner of my eye I noticed the man in the yellow raincoat. He was also sitting near the front, but now he was alone. His woman friend was seated in the back with Gretchen, talking.

I didn't know whether it was because Malcolm and James were there or because for the first time in hours I was warm, but suddenly I was not depressed anymore. The shed felt cozy. I saw Dorothy, Elaine, and Francis sitting together, my dear friends, my almost-family. It didn't matter what it was doing outside, inside we were safe.

The room became quiet and we began. The director stood next to me and gave me a long, flattering introduction. It was only the second time I'd read, so I was not used to people talking about me while I was present. I didn't know where to look, how to arrange my face while listening to such praise. I smiled at the ceiling, feeling pleased and slightly embarrassed.

Finally, she finished, and I started to read. Right away I noticed that something was happening, something was different. As I read, I recalled what singers and actors often say about an audience—that they can sense if it is responsive, if there is a connection. Whatever that connection was, it was in this shed.

When I finished, there was a series of questions. Most were about the writing process—why I had written the book, what it had been like trying to sell it. Several people were writers who spoke about their own books, their own publishing experiences. Among them was a well-known historian who didn't say anything, but he was attentive. His presence was a little unsettling. I wondered what he thought of my quiet, slender volume. I doubted that he had read it. Sitting beside him was his wife. I imagined she had brought him here to help support the sanctuary because she loved animals.

Some of the questions were more personal than I'd expected. How much had I been paid for the book? Had I sold the paperback rights? Had there been movie offers? I answered them honestly. I felt like I could tell them anything.

When the questions ended, people lined up to buy the book. I talked to each person as I signed his or her copy and thanked them for coming, for supporting the sanctuary on such a miserable day. All the proceeds from the sale of the book would go to the sanctuary. Out of the corner of my eye, I saw the man in the yellow raincoat waiting. He apparently wanted to be last.

Finally, there was no one left in line. People were milling about the shed, talking to each other. No one seemed to be leaving. The man in the raincoat came up to where I was still sitting in my chair at the front of the room. Standing in front of me, smiling, he reached out and cradled my face in his hand. "You are precious," he said, "so open and honest. I knew I had to meet such a woman."

I was flabbergasted. I didn't know what to say. I couldn't remember ever being touched this way and by a stranger. By a man. I said something banal. *Thank you. That's nice. Really?* I was confused.

"My name is Dennis Stock," he said and took my hand, placing it between both of his and holding it there.

Dennis Stock?

"I bought your house," I said. This was totally unbelievable. "Twenty-four years ago, I bought my house from you."

We stared at each other, smiling in our confusion and delight at this wild coincidence. Then Dennis started to laugh. He threw his head back and laughed loud and hard. I was laughing, too. It was so outrageous. So weird.

I couldn't connect the man in front of me with the man I remembered from the closing. It had been too long ago, and we'd aged too much, apparently beyond recognition. But I distinctly remembered how I'd felt about the man whose house I was buying then, and it hadn't been good. He'd seemed arrogant and controlling. He was selling his house and moving to France that very day. He'd rushed us through the closing so he could get to the airport to catch his plane to Paris. He was intimidatingly handsome, overwhelmingly smart, and on top of that he was a world-renowned photographer and actually sort of famous. I owned two of his books. I even had a poster of one of his photographs framed on the wall of my office. I remembered thinking that no one like that would ever be interested in someone like me.

He let go of my hand to pick up a book. "Please sign it," he said, handing it to me. While I was writing, he talked to me. "Is this man, Hank, still in the picture?" he asked. The passage I had just read referred to the beginning of a relationship I'd had with a man named Hank.

"If I tell you, it will spoil the ending of the book," I replied. I was done writing and handed the book back to him.

He laughed and opened the book to see what I had written. "To Dennis, with best wishes from your housemate," he read aloud. He looked up, smiling broadly. "What a very interesting thing you suggest," he said.

"It's not a suggestion," I told him. "We simply share a house in a strange sequential way."

"But that's not what it says." He smiled, closing the book.

I was embarrassed and confused because in a way he was right. I'd written something provocative as an inscription. But it wasn't like me to flirt. Especially in writing.

He produced a piece of paper from his pocket and handed it to me. "Please write down your particulars," he said. "E-mail, phone, cell phone."

His confidence—pushiness—astounded me. "I'm leaving tomorrow on a two-month book tour," I told him while writing down the requested information. It was the truth but not the whole truth. I would be back and forth throughout the summer, but I didn't mention this. Somehow I felt as if I needed to put a big space between me and this man.

"That's OK," he said. "I'll be traveling, too, to London and Paris and then possibly to Italy. But I'd like for us to stay in touch, if you don't mind."

At that moment it wasn't clear to me whether I minded or not. I thought of the man who'd sat across from me at the closing twenty-four years ago. I looked at the handsome face in front of me now and suddenly I grabbed the pile of money from the cigar box and start counting it.

"Four hundred dollars," I announced to him when I was finished. "We raised four hundred dollars." I hoped I had changed the subject.

"You're a beautiful woman," he said.

Oh my God. Is this really happening?

I was silent in the car driving home with Dorothy. I dropped her at her house and half an hour later walked into my own, the house I'd lived in for twenty-four years. It was close to nine o'clock. I was nervous and fidgety and decided to call my friend Patti in Maine. I told her about my day at the sanctuary, about Franklin the pig. And then I told her about Dennis Stock. I explained about the house. I explained about his arrogance that day at the closing. I described what he looked like.

"Susan," she said in a funny voice when I was done. "What's going on?"

And even though I had no idea, I told her the one thing I knew for sure.

"Something big," I said.

I WAS TALKING TO Steve Cook, the director of the Starr Library in Rhinebeck, about stocking my book and hosting a reading there.

"An excerpt will be in the June issue of *O*," I told him, uncomfortable because this sounded like a sales pitch. I'd been driving around to small-town libraries all day, introducing myself and telling librarians about the book. Of all the book-publishing fantasies I'd had over the years, seeing my book in a library had been the strongest and most enduring. A library says it all: books matter, you're a writer, there is a shelf life beyond death.

"Oh?" Steve looked decidedly curious. "The new issue just came," he said, turning to a table behind him and riffling through a stack of unopened mail. He pulled out the latest edition of *O, The Oprah Magazine* and slid it across the counter to me.

Another librarian, a woman, who'd overheard me say "Oprah," came over. The three of us leaned on the counter as I flipped through the pages to the book section. There were four or five full- and half-page book reviews, all with photos, but I saw nothing for my book. I flipped back and forth through the book section several times. No excerpt.

"I'm *sure* my publisher said June," I mumbled. I knew I

should have kept my mouth shut about *Oprah* until I'd seen it myself. This is what I got for jumping the gun. I consulted the index and noticed the heading *One Is the Loneliest Number* under Features. I wrote about loneliness, could the excerpt be there? I looked. Nothing.

"I'm so embarrassed," I said out loud as the woman drifted away. But I kept going back to the book section again and again, as if the excerpt might miraculously appear.

Steve stayed at the counter, apparently still friendly. "We'd love to schedule a reading," he said, ignoring the possibility that I had just told a whopper.

"There!" I bent closer over the page. It *was* in the book section, a very short excerpt. No photo but it was there. Page 188.

Steve's female colleague returned and the three of us leaned over the magazine as if we were looking for a dropped contact lens.

"That's terrific," Steve said, as if size didn't matter.

It was one of those schizophrenic moments in getting published.

It's in O!

It's so *missable!*

I left the library feeling at once elated and ashamed. I'd been saved from a lie but barely. How had my book ended up in *O* anyway? Someone must have liked it enough to excerpt it, but then not enough to include a photo, not even of the cover. Life is full of mixed messages. This was another one.

I had one more library to visit, the one in my own town of Olivebridge. It was out in the middle of nowhere, an hour's drive from the library in Rhinebeck. I never went to my local library. It was thirty minutes from my house in the opposite direction of where I worked, grocery shopped, and banked. I felt guilty about this but with the recent gas crunch not as guilty as I used to. Still, asking them to carry my book felt a little hypocritical when I had done nothing to support them.

But after I introduced myself, the librarian there shook my hand and said of course they'd carry the book. She didn't mention that she'd never seen me before. A lot of New York City people have weekend homes in this vicinity, so maybe she thought I was one of them. I didn't mention *O*. Out here in the middle of the woods in the Catskill Mountains, that kind of self-promotion seemed especially false—and, besides, the excerpt had been so tiny, hardly worth mentioning.

After going to every library within an hour of my house, I arrived home to twenty-six e-mails. None of them were spam. I never used to get twenty-six e-mails in one week. Another sign of how much my life had changed. For almost ten years I had worked to simplify my life, to eliminate nonessential activities in order to have time to write. That meant dropping out of my reading and women's groups, both of which I'd been part of for more than seven years. It meant no longer teaching classes on weekends or at night. It meant dropping my gym membership and, instead, getting a treadmill so I could save time by exercising at home. It meant letting my subscriptions to the *New Yorker, National Geographic,* and my local newspaper lapse. It meant spending less time with friends. It meant turning off my phone when I wrote or when I needed time to think. It meant I had become more and more isolated. I didn't know how else to do it, to nurture and protect my decision to write.

Some of my friends had been upset with me for years,

years of my not returning phone calls or not returning them soon enough, years of hearing "I can't make it" too often. I'd become an absent friend. Somehow I'd hoped they'd hang in there anyway. And most had. Still, twenty-six e-mails was part of the new reality, part of my reemergence into the world of two-way communication. Some were from well-wishing friends or relatives who had just heard the news. Some were from my editor or agent. One from my publicist said, "The book will be in the June issue of *People*, too. That gives you *O* and *People*."

How do you respond to that? For the first time the exclamation key on my computer started to show signs of use.

I knew that *People* had been considering a review of the book. Soho had sent them a galley and we heard back in January that they wanted photos of me with a horse. Since I no longer had my own horse, I arranged with my friend Margaret to have pictures taken with her Friesian gelding, Rinza. He was a magnificent animal, with a wavy black mane down to his knees and a black tail that swept behind him like a wedding train. It was impossible not to fall in love with Rinza. He was huge and gentle and fortunately had enough star wattage for both of us. He possessed exactly the kind of glamour you'd expect to find in *People*. I did not. But horses always make humans look better and Rinza helped me relax, which was reflected in the beautiful photographs taken of us. We e-mailed the photos to my publicist, who forwarded them to *People*, and then for months we heard nothing. I assumed *People* had lost interest or had never had much in the first place and had forgotten about it. Then a second request came in May. In the photographs we had taken in January, I was wearing a parka. Since the review would appear in the

June issue, could I send new photos ASAP *without* a parka? The trouble was, Rinza was gone, sent to Florida for dressage school. I'd have to find another horse, one as spectacular as Rinza. But I realized I didn't know another horse that magnificent, so I decided it would be OK to do something completely different—me in my own backyard, looking over the fence at my slightly muddy Appaloosa boarder, Chet. We spent a couple of hours taking new photos. I wore a rose-colored long-sleeved T-shirt, black jeans, and a pair of green Wellington boots. No jewelry, no makeup, no flashy horse to make up for the unflashy human leaning against the fence. In the photos, the pasture behind me was verdant, the sky deep blue, and while Chet isn't flashy, she's a lovely horse.

I liked everything about the pictures except me. There I was, in the middle of all that spring splendor, an aging, overweight woman, lifting a lined, jowly—though smiling—face into the morning sun. I wanted not to care. I wanted to be dispassionate and unself-conscious about my aging self. I wanted to be a role model for my female students, for my beloved niece, Marguerite, for any young woman who might fear aging in an ageist culture. What mattered was living a purposeful life. Aging was what happened while you were busy doing something more important.

Instead, as I looked at the photographs later on the computer, for a moment I was full of self-loathing. I cringed and wished I could have been published ten years earlier. Who was I kidding? This was America. Looks mattered. Age mattered. I was sending a bunch of photographs of me to one of the most image-obsessed magazines in the world, which had once informed readers that Renée Zellweger had *ballooned* to 130 pounds to play the role of the overweight, overaged single woman Bridget Jones in the film of the same name. *Ballooned.* Few women could escape the implication, certainly not me, who had ballooned beyond 130 pounds and appeared to be ballooning still.

"IS YOUR HAIR thinning?" I asked Stephanie. Stephanie, Alex, Dorothy, and I were sitting around my dining-room table, eating grilled salmon and salad. On the table were four silver candlesticks that belonged to a great-grandmother I had never met. It was an early spring evening and not quite dark but I'd lit the candles anyway. I liked their incongruity on my small rustic table in my small rustic house where half the walls were old gray barn board. The candlelight cast a yellow glow on Stephanie's almost pure white hair. Parted on the side, it fell straight and sleek to her shoulders. Stephanie has a *People* magazine face. Men turn to look at Stephanie.

"God, yes," she said, as if the thinning of her hair were obvious. It wasn't but I'd noticed that my own hair had thinned and I wanted to know if it was happening to them, too.

"What about you?" I asked Dorothy, who has Farrah Fawcett hair without the side wings.

"Definitely," she nodded, but I couldn't tell with hers either. It looked thick and lush.

"Mine, too," said Alex, running her hands through a blonde, chin-length pageboy.

This launched us into a discussion about osteoporosis, colonoscopies (who'd had one, who hadn't), hormone replacement therapy, memory problems, insomnia, wrinkles, and weight gain. Stephanie and Alex are thin. Dorothy and I had both gained between ten and fifteen pounds over the past year. We were embarrassed by this and felt on some level that it was just one more way we'd been betrayed by our bodies. It was part of the shock of thinning hair, bad knees, and insomnia that went with leaving the age of fifty behind. I definitely should have been published ten years earlier.

When my cup of self-hatred had runneth over, Alex said, "*Excuse me,* but will everyone with an ISBN number please stand up!"

MY FRIENDS HAVE been wonderful at bolstering me. Sometimes it has been an uphill battle. I felt hated as a child. I don't know if it was real or not but it was real to me. It's been the hardest thing about my childhood to escape and sometimes it's clear I haven't. Therapy helped but I found something better: doing meaningful work. It's impossible to think about myself when I'm in a class with twenty students.

I had a two-year-old pug named Emma who became very sick in the summer of 2002. Over the period of a week, as the vet tried to diagnose the problem, it became clear that she was dying. It was July and I was teaching summer school at Ulster County Community College. I'd get up in the morning with a knot in my stomach and call the vet to see if Emma was still alive. Then I'd drive to school, crying, to teach a writing class. On the eight-mile drive to the college, I'd think about going to the veterinary hospital to be with Emma instead. Or I'd think about going home and crawling into bed and pulling the covers over my head. It was impossible to imagine that I would be able to teach a class on the importance of including a thesis statement in the first paragraph of an analysis essay. Who cared? My precious Emma was dying.

Then I'd arrive at my class.

There'd be twenty students sprawled in desks around the

room, each a story, a different kind of person. A few were teenagers; one, a single mother; another, a mature student working on a degree in education. In less than five minutes I would no longer be thinking about Emma. I would not be thinking about aging or feeling fat. The part of me that thought about me would be *gone*. Self-absorption, self-pity, fear, anxiety, doubt—they all vanished.

At the end of the week, Emma died of pug encephalitis. I was crazy with grief. On Monday morning I sat on the edge of my bed looking at Emma's toys still scattered around the floor, her little dog bed next to me on my own bed. I knew I couldn't go to class. I couldn't possibly teach. My eyes were red and swollen from crying. I'd hardly slept in two days.

Then I thought about my students. I saw them sitting at their desks with their essays out ready to read, talking to each other, waiting for class to start. I saw Tony, from campus security, walking into class to tell them I wasn't coming, that they could go home. They would be happy, in a way, to have the unexpected free summer morning. But my absence would send a message: whatever I was doing was more important than being with them. Is that what I wanted to say? Is that how I felt?

I dragged myself to class.

Five minutes after I got there, we were listening to an essay about a young man who lives in a small dark room and talks to a witty character named Death, who lives on the other side of his bedroom door. It was funny and macabre, with good writing and good, pithy dialogue. I wasn't thinking about Emma. I was no longer aware of my broken heart. I wasn't fat or old or possibly going bald. And if I had been, my students wouldn't have cared.

Neither would my horses have cared, nor my dogs or my Siamese. Perhaps that is why we humans are so devoted to animals, because they are not turned off by the outward appearances people so often judge us by. We may love horses for their sheer beauty but I don't think they fall in love with us for ours. Nor do they need to know how much we have achieved or how we rank on a best-seller list. They accept us for who we are. And so do my students. This is the real gift of teaching, of doing work that matters. My students almost never fail to engage me, to lift my spirits. Over and over again, I'd walk into a classroom and find myself transformed by their intelligence, their humor, and sometimes by their charm. And just as with horses, I am not always sure of how my students feel about me, but there has never been any question of my admiration and affection for them. Aging? Ballooning? Grieving? The answer is always the same and it always works. Teach. Because in the end, students are what matter.

{ 5 }

I WOKE UP EARLY and for a few minutes lay in bed with my eyes closed, luxuriating in the sweet cacophony of spring. There were the cries of the killdeer as they flew over the pasture, where they would lay their speckled eggs, perfectly camouflaged by a lichen-covered rock; the rapid chatter of two pairs of hummingbirds, newly returned from South America, nesting in the grove of bamboo growing outside my bedroom. They buzzed back and forth under my window to the sugar-water feeders hanging around the corner on the deck. Territorial and ferocious, they would dive-bomb the pugs, who dared to share that sunny space. Through a skylight above my head I could hear and watch swallows, cartwheeling through the air in screeching pursuit of bugs. A pair of red-tailed hawks lived in the old apple orchard behind the pond. They circled over the hay fields, the sounds of their high-pitched whines mingling with the chorus of crows and blue jays, in raucous pursuit, protesting their presence. The country in spring is not a quiet place.

I kept my eyes closed because as soon as I opened them, Lucy, my chocolate Lab, would creep up from the foot of the bed, where she had slept, to snuggle. She'd collapse her seventy-five pounds along my side, squishing one or both of the pugs lying next to me under the covers. My two pugs,

Luna and Noche, would scramble out from under her, surfacing near my head, where my Siamese cat, Sebastian, lay, all or part of him curled on my pillow. Eight pairs of eyes would stare at me (I can *feel* this even with my own firmly shut) to see if my eyes were open, the signal for the pugs to twirl in ecstasy all over the bed in anticipation of breakfast.

"Do your pugs twirl?" another pug owner I met on the street once asked. It's one of the most frequently asked questions among pug owners. Apparently, there are two kinds of pugs, those that twirl and those that don't. I can't imagine the latter. Mine twirl everywhere, for any reason, all over the bed at the sight of an open eye at five in the morning, all around my legs at the sound of their food dishes being taken down from on top of the refrigerator, at the sight of anything I pick up that might or might not signal a game of fetch, such as removing the mail from the mailbox. They twirl at the window when they spot anything that moves: squirrels, deer, leaves, things I can't see.

I live in dread of the day's first twirl because it is performed all over my chest, my stomach, and occasionally my face. There is no stopping it once it starts. I can either curl into a ball under the covers to protect myself or get up. Sebastian is a twirling victim, too, forced to abandon the pillow and escape to the windowsill above the bed where he will watch in disgust. Lucy loves it and lies on her back, biting gently at the dancing legs as they tumble across her.

I got up and tripped toward the bathroom as they took their twirling to the floor, around and through my legs. They grunted and snorted like baby pigs and barked at each other in that peculiar muffled voice pugs have. *Moof!* They don't sound like dogs. They don't behave like dogs. The truth is, they don't look much like dogs either; the undog dogs, the most primate-like of any canine breed I've known. They're laugh-out-loud funny. I called them my monkeys, my frogs, my bugs.

Lucy, my Lab, is the real dog. She has a face. Her eyes point in the same direction. It doesn't sound like she's underwater when she barks. She stops whatever she's doing when I say no. She would never walk across my face. She wouldn't eat five pounds of rotten crab apples and blow up like a beach ball and have to be driven to the emergency clinic at 3:00 a.m. to have her stomach pumped, and then do it again the very next day. She wouldn't think a horse, something that weighs half a ton more than she does, is a good thing to nip. She wouldn't twirl.

As I stumbled with the undogs underfoot, a knot formed in my stomach before I remembered why. It was Tuesday, May 23, the day I was to leave for a reading in Amherst, Massachusetts. It was the official beginning of the book tour. I would be away from home, the dogs, the cat, the horse, my quiet country life, my morning writing. But there was something more. What else was wrong? I scanned my memory, an unreliable tool in this age of menopause. But there it was, the flashing red strobe, the big new danger: Dennis Stock. *Oh God, I gave him my phone number, my e-mail address.*

I headed for the kitchen in search of Prilosec. I was ruining my health with anxiety. I knew I should meditate or take up yoga or run myself silly on the treadmill. Anything other than taking a pill to quell this new level of angst. I was beginning to understand that my reaction to good fortune was the same as to bad: fear. Even my friends didn't get it. Actually, neither did I. When I thought about it, when I took a deep breath and had a little talk with myself, I could feel satisfaction, the pride and joy of accomplishment. I just couldn't sustain it. Somehow the good feelings slipped away and anxiety returned.

"What are you afraid of?" Elaine had asked with an unmistakable edge of annoyance in her voice. When something nice happens in Elaine's life she is grateful, appreciative, and happy. She doesn't wring her hands, anticipating the disaster that will take it all away.

Even that question overwhelmed me. The afraid-of list was so long—endless really—as new things to be afraid of popped up daily. But what it boiled down to was the fear that I would die alone and broke in a seedy, state-run nursing home after living a largely meaningless life.

But first I had to get myself to Food for Thought Books in Amherst by 6:00 p.m. On top of the usual worries about leaving the house and the animals and wondering if anyone would come to the reading, I worried about what it would be like to see my ex-boyfriend, Paul, for the first time in four years. He was driving to Amherst from New York City to attend the reading. He would be staying with his good friend the author Norton Juster and Norton's wife, Jeanne, who live in Amherst and would also be coming to the reading. Afterward, the four of us had planned to have dinner.

The possibilities for disaster were myriad. Although Paul and I had parted amicably, we hadn't stayed in touch, which was mostly my fault. I'm terrible about returning phone calls, especially from people who aren't part of my daily circle. But also it had been painful to end a relationship with someone I still cared about in many ways and, at least initially, I needed time alone to make the transition to mere friendship. Even now, four years later, I didn't know what it would be like to see him again. Would I still feel sad about the loss of *us?* What if he told me about a new relationship? Would I feel terrible? Happy? Indifferent? I didn't know. By not staying in touch, I'd avoided feeling anything. Tonight I would have to feel something.

Norton Juster is one of the funniest people I know. He cringes when I tell him *The Phantom Tollbooth* was my favorite childhood book because it reminds him that he is twenty years older than I. A present I like to give friends for birthdays or Christmas is another book he wrote called *The Dot and the Line.* When I first met Paul and heard that his friend of thirty years and one-time partner in an architectural firm was Norton Juster, the author groupie in me burst forth.

I credit four authors for helping me through those tough early years: Frances Hodgson Burnett, Kay Thompson, Joy Adams, and Norton Juster. During the six years that Paul and I were together, I rarely spoke to Norton about my writing, in spite of the fact that in that time I completed three books and the first draft of a fourth. I wanted to talk to him about writing, but I wouldn't let myself. The reason was simple: he was a real writer and I wasn't. Where Norton was concerned, part of me would always be ten, and the author of *The Phantom Tollbooth* would always be a godlike entity. My ten-year-old self had difficulty imagining that entity coming to hear me read from my memoir.

I brought my suitcase up from the basement and put it on the bed. But first I took a shower. Afterward, I found both pugs and the cat in the suitcase with Lucy lying across the open lid. I was stricken with guilt and just plain sadness that they weren't coming with me. For a moment I stood next to the bed and soaked up the sight of my color-coordinated brood tucked into my luggage. One black, two beige, and a chocolate: almost a Burberry motif. Except for Lucy, they were bunched together so tightly it looked like one animal with three heads.

I dreaded this separation so much that I had briefly considered renting an RV for the summer and bringing them on the tour with me. But the logistics seemed daunting. Lucy needs a swim every day. I saw myself with the unwieldy rig driving on small back roads somewhere in New England searching for a lake or a pond, any place legal for Lucy to swim in. Say we found a pond and Lucy had a delirious hour of fetching the stick I threw out as far into the water as I could. The pugs would go into the water, too. Luna swims almost as well as Lucy, but Noche wades up to his chest and screams at Luna and Lucy swimming away from him, making a sound best described by someone once as an angry parrot.

When the swim was over, it would be time to go back to the RV. What had seemed like a big vehicle would be suddenly claustrophobic as it filled with the smell of wet dog. Naturally, everybody would head for the bed, which in the canine mind doubles as a towel. It's the logical place to roll after a bracing swim in pond scum and, besides, it's the perfect place to stand at the big window and bark maniacally at dogs riding in passing cars. It's also the ideal place to twirl.

Later I would stand at the front of a bookstore in a crisp white linen shirt and khaki-colored cargo pants, pocked from neck to knees with shaking-wet-dog water marks, smelling of the same, and read to an audience of two: the owner of the bookstore, her assistant, and several rows of empty chairs.

Much later, parked under the glow of a buzzing parking-lot light, I would fall asleep between damp sheets, pinned by Lucy stretched across my legs, only to be wakened regularly by the pugs, twirling across my chest.

I decided against renting an RV. Instead, a young woman named Kristen would house-sit. I had typed up five single-spaced pages of instructions for her. Most of the directives had to do with taking care of the pugs, who I was sure would self-destruct the minute I turned my back. This was not entirely unfounded. There was that crab-apple incident, in duplicate. And once there had been something worse.

I had been working on the computer one night, completely absorbed in what I was doing, when Luna staggered into the office and collapsed on my foot. Her eyes rolled into the back of her head and her body went completely rigid. I had been so focused on my work that I had no idea what she'd been doing or where she had been doing it. Without even thinking, I reached down her throat to see if her airway was blocked. It was, and I pulled out a thick wad of soggy rawhide bone.

The incident terrified me. What if she hadn't been able to get my attention? What if I hadn't been home? What if I hadn't guessed what to do quickly enough? Afterward, I held her and cried. I wrote a letter to the manufacturer, and I called the pet shop to tell them of the incident. But rawhide bones are still sold everywhere and letting your dog have one is like encouraging her to chew on a land mine.

AT 2:00 P.M. I pulled out of the driveway for the two-and-a-half hour drive to Amherst, the start of the tour that would take me through parts of New York, Massachusetts,

Connecticut, Rhode Island, Maine, New Hampshire, and Vermont. I felt incredibly alone, as though I were going out to face the real world by myself for the first time. This was what happened if you got what you asked for. You got to have it. All of it. As nervous as I was about living alone among strangers for two months, I was more nervous about seeing friends and relatives again, some of whom I hadn't laid eyes on in thirty-five years. Months ago I had mass-mailed a postcard of the book jacket and my reading dates to everyone I knew or had ever known. Many responded and, beginning tonight, I would be getting together with them on every day of the tour. In spite of the anxiety I felt about reconnecting with people from the past from whom I had consciously separated myself, I was well aware that by sending out the postcards, I had initiated it. I'd sent them not only to help the book succeed but because connecting with these people after years of silence was the next step I needed to take as a person.

Just before five, I checked into the Lord Jeffery Inn, a brick colonial structure in the middle of town, right next to Amherst College. The name Lord Jeffery hadn't meant anything to me but when I saw the inn, I remembered I'd been there, forty-three years before, to be exact.

I had just started eighth grade at Northampton School for Girls, which was located not far from Amherst. A grandmother I hardly knew, my mother's mother, who lived in Geneva, Switzerland, had come to see me at the school unannounced. She'd brought me here to this inn for lunch. I'd sat across the table from this attractive stranger, staring at her red hair and jewelry. I'd never seen anyone so glamorous except in a magazine. We hardly spoke, but in the middle of lunch she suddenly unclasped one of the bracelets from her wrist and reached across the table to put it on mine. It was a gold charm bracelet and as she settled it on my wrist, she briefly explained what every charm meant to her. They all had something to do with places or things she loved, mostly things about Switzerland: a Swiss cowbell, a gondola with a door that opened, a poodle, a Swiss coin, a mountaineering backpack, a raised profile of the Matterhorn Mountain on a disk, and my favorite, a little gold bidet. After lunch she took me back to school and I didn't see her again until I was twenty-three. She was still glamorous, still a stranger, and we didn't know what to say to each other. It was the last time I saw her, although she would live another ten years.

Standing in the lobby, I was filled with the memory of that visit and of the two years I'd spent at Northampton School for Girls, a place I loved because it was the first time I had felt kindness, the first time not having parents didn't matter because no one had parents while they were at school. It was the first place I lived where I felt wanted, by teachers who were nurturing and by the other students, some of whom I grew to love like sisters. Northampton was a home to me, and I dreaded leaving to spend holidays with my real relatives.

I dropped my suitcase in my room on the second floor and went off to explore the town and find the Food for Thought bookstore. It was a clear spring evening as I cut across the large town common where students were playing Frisbee and sitting scattered across the grass in small groups, talking.

To be in Amherst is to be in the presence of Emily Dickinson. I wandered around town in my Emily Dickinson mode and found two bookstores in addition to the one where I was to read. Neither carried my book. I was disappointed but not surprised. A memoir centered around horses by a first-time author? When I thought of it that way, why would anyone carry it? Still, the disappointment lingered, and I wondered if this summer I would be walking in and out of bookstores all over New England that had elected not to carry the book. This was exactly what I had feared most. After all the years of rejections, I would finally sell a book and out it would go into the world of critics, bookstores, and readers, where it would get the equivalent of a giant shrug. *Good try, dear, but you're going to have to do a whole lot better than this if you want to be taken seriously.*

I spotted the bookstore where I would be reading in about an hour. From the perspective of someone momentarily filled with shame and self-loathing, it looked awful: the least attractive, worst-located, most unbookstorish store in the whole town. It was the store most likely to carry a bunch of loser authors no one had ever heard of. Never mind that the truth was it was a large, well-stocked, attractive space, four doors away from the dead center of town. I looked in the window but didn't go in. Taped to the glass front door was a small notice about the reading at 6:00 p.m. Except for one or two young women behind the counter, there was no one in the store.

I hurried back to the Lord Jeffery Inn with renewed certainty that I was the wrong person to send on a book tour. Lots of authors never go on tour and, clearly, I should have been one of them.

"There will be times when hardly anyone will show up at a reading," my agent, Helen, had warned me once. "But you'll never get less than two," she'd added.

Two?

I was in crisis mode as I changed clothes. I'd packed five

white linen shirts and two pairs of khaki cargo pants. In eliminating choice, I had at least eliminated anxiety about what to wear. I was left with anxiety about seeing Paul, reading in front of Norton, and addressing a lot of empty chairs.

It was time to go. I walked across the common again, through laughing students still sprawled in groups across the grass, through a town full of people coming and going on this perfect spring evening. Anxiety is the most isolating feeling I know, a bubble of self-centered fear so impenetrable it can easily keep out something as flimsy as reality. Since there is no reasoning with anxiety, I've learned the only thing to do is to take a deep breath and act as if nothing is wrong.

A few minutes before six, I walked into a virtually empty Food for Thought Books. Two young women stood behind a counter piled high with my books. Twenty folding chairs were arranged in rows of five in the middle of the store and behind us was a table with food, wine, and coffee. I introduced myself to the women behind the counter. They were friendly and said nice things about the book.

"There are a lot of horse people in the area," one said. "We're expecting a good turnout."

I was still talking to them when Paul, Norton, and Jeanne walked into the store. When I saw them it was as though no time had passed, as though we had all been together just the week before. It was strange and enjoyable. We hugged each other, laughing because Norton was already making jokes, probably about Paul, whom he loves to tease. I felt a deep affection for Paul, remembering all the things I liked about him, including his large dark twinkling eyes. The four of us made a little circle with the folding chairs and sat down to catch up on the last four years.

* * *

THE ENTIRE TIME Paul and I had been together I had been writing and trying to publish. As we sat and talked, it occurred to me that I must have been a difficult partner as I struggled to cope with constant rejections. Paul had always been a willing reader and claimed to like all my books. I had accused him of not being critical enough and, because of that, I never valued his opinion.

"But tell me what you *don't* like," I'd say after hearing him praise a particular manuscript.

"Well," he'd reply, looking trapped, "I can't really think of anything."

"*That doesn't help me,*" I'd say, exasperated. He was so smart. If he'd just tell me what was wrong, if somebody would, I could fix it and sell a book. Poor Paul. Dinners could be tough. It was a miracle he was still talking to me, let alone had driven for almost three hours to hear me read from a book he'd read once in manuscript form and had had the audacity to say he liked.

BY A QUARTER past six, with fewer than fifteen people in the audience, the manager of the bookstore apologized for the poor attendance but suggested we begin.

To someone predisposed to feeling marginalized, reading in front of a lot of empty chairs presents a challenge. I told myself it was my spiritual path, my life's lesson to come to terms with the times when no one showed up. I told myself the people who mattered were there: Norton, Jeanne, and Paul. I told myself to just read. I did, and everything went smoothly. People laughed. People bought books. I signed them. Norton said something funny and we laughed some more. Everything was OK. My anxiety had passed and I was left with a feeling of pure gratitude that the book had given me the courage to do this, to reconnect with people I'd loved and to meet new people who shared a love of books and horses.

Afterward, Paul and I held hands as we walked toward the restaurant. It felt like the most natural thing in the world. We were too early for our dinner reservation so, to kill time, the four of us wandered around town and finally went into one of the bookstores that didn't carry my book but did have Norton's new children's book, *The Hello, Goodbye Window*.

When we finally sat down to eat it was almost nine o'clock and I was exhausted. I was happy to be in the presence of three such dear friends. It was the first time I'd felt relaxed all day.

WITH THE FIRST day of the tour over, it seemed like a major hurdle was behind me. One down, sixty to go. I'd survived seeing Paul. I'd survived a low turnout at the reading. I'd survived two out of three bookstores not carrying my book. In a little while, I'd survive sleeping without my dogs, maybe the hardest thing yet.

I felt sad as I walked across the common on the chilly spring night—that Paul and I hadn't worked out, that I might have hurt such a thoroughly decent man. But for all I knew, he was now madly in love with someone else. We had been careful not to ask each other anything about new interests. I tried to remember what it was like to be with him, why I had wanted out. I wanted to remember the bad parts so I wouldn't have to feel this sadness, this wedge of regret. There was the back and forth to the city, always leaving the animals, and both of us making work a priority: for him, architecture, and for me, writing. The good thing about Paul was that we could be apart when we were together, which meant we could both work. But I had realized ultimately that what mattered to Paul was his work. I had seen that work dominated our relationship and, in the end, even when we were together, what I really felt was alone. Perhaps he did, too.

Sadness clung to me the next morning as we caught up on news about family and mutual friends while holding hands across the breakfast table. Remembering we'd made a poor couple didn't diminish my gloom. He'd stopped working for two days to come see me. Well, not quite. He told me he was returning to the city after breakfast. If the traffic was OK, he'd be at his desk by one, less than twenty-four hours after he'd left. Still, he'd come. We had reconnected, and it felt good. Maybe we couldn't be a couple but I loved this man anyway. I would always love him.

Saying goodbye on the sidewalk later I made promises I wondered if I would keep. I said I would stay in touch. I said I would call when I was in the city. And as I was walking away, I waved and said, "I'll see you soon."

I DROVE EAST on the turnpike toward Salem, Massachusetts, headed toward a 7:00 p.m. reading at Feed Your Head Books and a reunion with my cousin Laura. We had once been very close but had drifted apart. I was headed toward a place full of memories. I missed the dogs. I missed my cat. I missed walking across the pasture at dawn with Lucy, to spend half an hour with the horse before going inside to begin the day's writing. I missed how safe I felt alone on my small farm, tucked far away from the past, good or bad.

But even home was changing; the safety I felt there, the solitude, was undergoing an alteration. It was not just because of the book and the flood of attention it had brought into my life. It was also because of a *man*. It was because of a disturbing e-mail from Dennis Stock.

{ 6 }

IN THE HAWTHORNE HOTEL in Salem, I sat in my room staring at my computer. It was two o'clock. I had to answer seventeen new e-mails before I could walk around town and then meet my cousin Laura, back at the hotel, at five.

The computer screen was filled with e-mails, some of which terrified me, like those from my roommates in prep school whom I hadn't seen in over thirty years, making final plans to meet me as I toured. Others were from Kathy at Soho, letting me know about the new bookstores she had added to the schedule. Still others were from relatives I barely knew who had read my book and wondered if they were the "bad" ones I'd portrayed. Some were from strangers, heartwarming e-mails about the book, sent to Soho and forwarded to me, and some were from horse rescue organizations, praising the book for helping to expose the plight of abused and neglected horses. They were from alcoholics who told me they, too, had stopped drinking. They were from women who had suffered domestic abuse. They were from people who had lost something they loved deeply: a child, an animal, a sibling. They were from my brother, still incredulous that I had sold a book, sharing every e-mail he had sent or received related to my publication. They were from a radio station in Utah that wanted to do an interview. They were from newspapers in Palm Beach, Los Angeles, Boston, Raleigh, and Kingston, New York, that wanted to do an interview. They were from my agent telling me which publisher had just rejected my novel and where she would send it next. They were from my friend and free-lance editor, Nan, who was reediting another of my novels. They were from my house sitter telling me flowers had come for the third time that week, from people I didn't know. They were from my dear friend Allie, whom I normally talked to on the phone almost every morning but who now e-mailed me instead. Gone were the days of confronting mostly spam, of silence stretching into the future indefinitely.

The scariest e-mail of all was from Dennis Stock. The morning I'd left for Amherst—was it really only two days ago?—I received my first e-mail from him. It was a photograph of him sitting next to his black Lab, Ty. Dennis was waving at the camera and his e-mail said, *We are looking forward to dinner with you.* He was leaving for Europe in mid-June and wanted to know if we could have dinner together before then.

I hadn't replied to his invitation and had instead asked if he was always so intense. The way he had touched my face at the reading, told me I was beautiful, and then sent me a photograph of himself felt almost intrusive. Certainly it felt intense. And now I'd received a second e-mail from him, responding to my question with this:

> Am I intense? That is a leading question. It depends on the circumstances. I can be very laid back in the settings that are appropriate to serenity or I can be excited and

passionate about the moment, place, or person that reveals truth and beauty in an unexpected place. I didn't have any preconceptions about the other afternoon and when I listened to your candidness, I knew I wanted to know you and that lit my fire. I am highly predisposed to those who try to be honest and coincidentally find inspiration in animals. After all, my first color essay many years ago was "The Land of St. Francis." Finally, I do believe in fate. So pack that in with blouses, pants, and bras and please keep me in mind as you hustle. May I also suggest that you don't tell the public how much you got as an advance on the book? You are just entering the first level of celebrity and the more your business life is kept private the better. You are special and you should defend that.

D

I had never received such a communication from a man. It was breathtaking in its straightforwardness, its eloquence, and its undisguised declaration of interest. I tried to remember if I'd ever been with a man who loved animals as I do, who found *inspiration* in them. Hank, whom I'd written about in *Chosen by a Horse,* was allergic to anything with fur, and Paul was indifferent to animals. When Allie and I talked about someone who didn't understand animals (and, therefore, shouldn't own them), we'd say, "He thinks they're livestock." Paul thought animals were livestock and had never been comfortable when any of mine had hopped onto his lap. In the six years we'd been together, he'd only been in my barn once.

Dennis Stock found inspiration in animals.

His fire had been lit.

He believed in fate.

Do I? Possibly. Someone advised me years ago to pay attention to the circumstances of your first meeting with someone because it can foretell the nature of the relationship. With Dennis, first I'd bought his house, and twenty-four years later we'd met again at an animal sanctuary.

At the very least, his e-mail required an equally straightforward response, and it wouldn't hurt if I could be eloquent, too. After all, he was the photographer, I was the writer. But when something made me this nervous, it was hard for me to tell how I felt, and to find the right words to express my feelings. Anxiety kills eloquence, so I ignored this latest e-mail and instead replied to Dennis's previous one, saying that the evening of Tuesday, May 30, might be possible for dinner if I was not too tired from driving. *I'll call you,* I said pointedly. As I clicked on *Send*, I felt as though I had just done something wildly reckless, something that would alter the course of my life forever.

I hurried through the rest of my e-mails, answering the essential ones but putting off most until later that night for something to do when insomnia set in.

It was warm and sunny as I crossed Hawthorne Boulevard— where a large bronze statue of Salem's most famous author, Nathaniel Hawthorne, stands—and walked several blocks toward the historic center of town.

If Amherst is Emily Dickinson, Salem is the witchcraft trials of 1692. As I walked the length of Salem's pedestrian mall, I passed shop after shop full of witch items: T-shirts embellished with every stereotype of witch images, mugs, wands, hats, wigs, capes, potions, black cats, etc. Trivializing these three-hundred-year-old murders troubled me. I'd felt the same way the first time I saw the Colosseum in Rome, where smiling tourists posed for pictures with costumed gladiators as though thousands of humans and animals hadn't been tortured and slaughtered on the very ground where vendors now sold plastic swords and helmets to eight-year-old boys. But Salem has taken pains to acknowledge the atrocities that took place there by establishing the Salem Witch Museum and the Salem Witch Trials Memorial, a landscaped walkway at one end of the pedestrian mall adjacent to the graveyard where some of the accused are buried.

I sat on a bench in the shade midway along the walk and imagined the terror that had gripped the town during the summer of 1692. I thought of Allie, a friend as dear to me as a sister and someone who, from the beginning, seemed as witchy to me as anyone I'd ever met, if being a witch meant possessing a profound capacity for love, insight, and healing.

Because of our work schedules, it was rare that Allie and I could find the time to spend a whole day together now although we'd been friends for twenty years. I knew where she hid her money. We were in each other's wills. She understood people and horses better than anyone I knew.

We'd met because of her voice.

Four years after I'd bought my house I'd been a full-time student in graduate school getting a master's degree in social work. I was struggling to pay the tuition and decided to advertise for a housemate. As soon as the ad came out in the paper I knew it was a bad idea. I couldn't possibly share my small house with anyone. But it was too late. The phone had already started ringing.

"I'm sorry," I said to callers, "the room's been rented." I must have said it a dozen times that morning. Then the phone rang again.

"I need a place to live while I finish building my house," the woman explained. "Probably no more than six months." Her voice was low and rich, the way people spoke in old movies. It was slightly husky, slightly smoky, slightly breathy. It was full of warmth and mischief. I felt I could tell this voice the truth.

"I changed my mind about a roommate," I said, "but I'd like to meet you anyway."

She came over and we sat on the back deck with my Siamese cat and my collie mix with the bad leg. My three horses grazed in the pasture a short distance away and swallows flew effortlessly over the surface of the pond plucking out bugs. While we talked she massaged the muscles of my dog's hind leg, the one she'd broken as a puppy when she'd jumped out of a moving truck, the reason she'd almost been euthanized by her first owners, who didn't think a dog was worth a vet's bill.

"Something's wrong with this dog," Allie said, moving her hands in circles around the dog's hip where the broken bone had once protruded.

I explained about the broken leg, the cast that had covered her from hip to toe.

"No," she said, shaking her head, "there's something else."

It was spooky and magical at the same time. The word "witch" came to mind.

A month later my dog almost died before they diagnosed her with lupus, an autoimmune disease that's not so rare in humans but quite rare in dogs.

I shudder to think what would have become of Allie in the Salem of 1692.

To SHAKE THE pall of gloom cast by thoughts of witch hangings, I went into the very modern Peabody Essex Museum to look at artifacts brought back from Asia by early colonial traders. On the way out I stopped in the gift shop to look for something to give Kristen as a thank you for house-sitting. I found a silver bracelet of linking horse heads and hoped it would be the perfect gift for a horse-crazy young woman.

Before heading back to the hotel to meet my cousin Laura, I pulled out the piece of paper with the address of Feed Your Head Books and headed to 272 Essex Street. It was only two blocks away on the same street as the museum, and when I found it, before going in, I stood before the window, surprised to see a display of nothing but my books. As far as I knew, this was the first bookstore that had devoted its entire front window (actually two windows—one on each side of the front door) to my book. In addition, there was a sandwich board (another first) placed on the sidewalk announcing my appearance later that night. Part of me wanted to rush off to buy a disposable camera to record this momentous occasion and part of me wanted to rush inside to warn the sweet-looking owner that she would bankrupt herself by featuring my book.

I walked into the store and introduced myself to the owner, who added to my emotional overload by telling me how much she loved *Chosen by a Horse*. She was so young that I was surprised she'd connected so strongly to a memoir written by a much older woman, especially when she told me she had no particular interest in horses. The store was tiny, no more than five or six hundred square feet, and in addition to the books displayed in the front windows, my book also was stacked inside. It looked as if she had staked the financial health of her store on the sale of this one book.

LAURA IS A ferocious reader; she ran out of bookshelf space in her apartment a long time ago. The last time I'd been there, stacks of books teetered on the floor in piles everywhere. It reminded me of the interior of the home of her great-uncle, Fred Robinson, a Chaucer scholar, translator, and one-time president of Radcliffe College. Located in Brattle Square in Cambridge, it featured stacks of books on the floor and on every table. I was nine when I first met Uncle Fritz, as his family called him, and he was in his eighties. I was living just outside of Boston with Laura's family that year, and we went to Uncle Fritz's for Thanksgiving. Two things about that day remain vivid. One was the surprise of seeing stacks of books like that in an otherwise traditionally furnished house, and the other was tasting turtle soup for the first time. The turtle soup was OK, but the books piled everywhere were fantastic, and I knew right then that I, too, wanted to be a collector of books. Laura would have been four that Thanksgiving. Perhaps she, too, fell in love with the stacks of books and now, more than forty years later, has reproduced the look of Uncle Fritz's house in her Somerville apartment.

I'd only stayed with Laura's family for a year before I was sent on to Baltimore to live with my maternal grandfather, and Laura and I hadn't become close until I moved back to Boston to attend graduate school at Brandeis in the summer of 1974 when I was twenty-three and Laura, nineteen. I have a photograph of her from that time standing halfway up a

ladder in the bookstore she worked in then, one hand holding onto the ladder, the other outstretched toward the camera with her incredible waist-length brown hair cascading
down her back. It is the photograph that best captures her
character for me: a smiling, intelligent face; the unfussed-
with gorgeous hair; and, of course, she is completely surrounded by books.

Those six years I lived in Boston were some of the best
but most difficult years of my life. I rented my first apartment and also was hired for my first job as a high-school
English teacher. It was the first time I really got to know my
brother, Lloyd, who lived nearby in the suburb of Wayland.
We had some crazy arguments then but what I remember
most is how much fun we had together and how glad I was
to finally live near him. With Lloyd, my aunt and uncle, and
their three daughters—Laura, Holly, and Christie—all living in or near Boston, I had the best of my family around me,
those who, after the loss of my parents, had done the most
to try to make me feel included. Several times a week I'd
get together with my aunt and uncle, or my brother, or Laura
or one of her sisters for dinner or a movie. On weekends in
the summer we'd go to the beach on Plum Island or drive to
New Hampshire or western Massachusetts to hike. And
every summer for two weeks I'd go with my aunt and uncle
and my three cousins to their summer house in Maine on
Little Cranberry Island.

But those were also the years when my panic attacks
began. They had started when I was about twenty, in college,
and by the time I was living in Boston, they were daily and
debilitating. Looking back, it is hard to imagine how I func-
tioned at all with the level of fear that gripped me from the

moment I woke up. Until I found a therapist, I kept these attacks a secret from everyone except my brother, who also suffered from anxiety. People who knew me then said I appeared to be a confident, fun-loving person. Recently, a friend sent me a copy of a letter I had written her in 1979. What impressed me about the letter was the same thing that struck me about how people described me. Both the letter and my seventies persona seemed so normal. There was no hint of how unhinged I felt, how anxiety-ridden. Apparently there was no obvious sign of it in my behavior either.

But the truth is, from my early twenties until I was almost forty years old, figuring out how to cope with anxiety trumped everything else. Anxiety (or fear—they were the same to me) was the controlling force in my life. I didn't need a reason to feel anxious, although there were times when my panic was precipitated by an actual event. But most of the time it wasn't connected to anything in particular. It was classic free-floating anxiety, known in the medical world as panic disorder.

I can look at almost any photograph of myself from those years and recall what level of anxiety I was experiencing the day the picture was taken. There is a photograph of me, Laura, and Laura's younger sister, Holly, sitting with our legs dangling over the seat of a giant chair sculpture we had climbed as it stood in front of a high school in western Massachusetts, a gift to the school from a recent graduating class. We had been driving back to Boston after a day of hiking when we spotted the huge chair and thought sitting in it together would make a funny picture. Today when I look at this picture of my smiling face, for me it is not a record of a silly moment I shared with my two cousins. Rather, it is a reminder of being trapped in the backseat of the car between Laura and Holly, taking deep breaths through a series of panic attacks, all the while pretending to feel fine. It was hard to know which was worse—the panic attacks or the shame I felt about experiencing something I neither understood nor could control.

I don't know why I wasn't given medication for anxiety. My therapist did prescribe Valium, but I knew it was addictive so I was afraid to take it. Knowing I had the Valium helped, though, so I carried the bottle with me everywhere but took pills so rarely that one bottle of twenty lasted more than ten years. I still have seven pills left in a bottle with an expiration date of 1982.

Anxiety was a terrible thing to live with because it spawned a number of related problems like suicidal thoughts, smoking, anorexia, and, finally, alcoholism. For some reason, my fear of addiction didn't apply to smoking and drinking. I went to great lengths to hide everything but my smoking, then socially acceptable, from my therapist. Outwardly, I seemed to be indistinguishable from any young recent graduate working at her first real job. Inwardly, I was a train wreck. I don't know how I survived. In some strange way, before my alcohol consumption became excessive, drinking actually helped me. The only relief I got from anxiety (besides the rare half a Valium I took) came when I was asleep or when I drank.

I had two serious relationships during my Boston years, both with smart, interesting men, both with unhappy endings. What surprises me now isn't that they ended, but that they happened at all. In one relationship, I lived with a man for four years and virtually every weekend I participated in something that terrified me almost more than anything else I could imagine.

My first date with this man remains at the top of my personal "most horrifying moments" list.

"I'll pick you up for dinner at four thirty," said the wonderful new voice on the phone. We'd met the weekend before at a party and had tumbled into a kind of love-at-first-sight craziness.

Dinner at that time seemed strangely early but this was the most attractive man in the world so what did I care if we ate it in the middle of the afternoon?

At four thirty his MG convertible pulled up to the curb in front of my apartment building and off we drove, further and further away from Boston, further and further away from the fancy, romantic restaurant I had imagined, perhaps somewhere along the waterfront with a dramatic view of the harbor—horribly, gratifyingly expensive. And me, so fetching in my tiny new dress with Pappagallo shoes to match. I was hoping relief was only minutes away in the shape of a bottle of Dom Pérignon, or a wonderful Sauterne. We were in love. Nothing was too extravagant.

But we went on. Pretty soon there were no more stores and no more restaurants. There were no more buildings at all as we rode along winding country roads lined with trees and fields. My anxiety increased until suddenly relief and joy swept over me. A picnic! We were going on the most romantic dinner of them all, a country picnic. Hidden in the trunk of his car was the special bottle of something along with a pretty basket filled with the gourmet foods I would appreciate, but not touch.

He turned right at a sign that said Hanscome Field and

pretty soon we arrived at a small airport. I gave another sigh of relief as I realized that somewhere in the miniature terminal in front of which he had parked the car must be the special restaurant that only this wonderful man knew about. I hopped out, his perky, smiling date, careful not to mention that I needed a drink from that bottle of whatever it was in the trunk of his car *right now.*

The rest is a blur, a heart-pounding, temple-throbbing blur. He grabbed my hand, strode toward the line of small planes parked on the tarmac, and shoved me into the passenger seat in the cockpit of one of them. Why didn't I object? Why did I allow myself to be subjected to this most terrifying activity? It grieves me today to think of how unable I was then to say no to something that scared me that much. It's one thing to push yourself through a fear, it's another thing to feel you might die doing it.

"I like to chase sunsets," he said with a smile, as we flew into the agoraphobia-inducing expanse of red and pink sky.

I survived an hour of teeth-chattering, gerbil-minded fright before he landed in a grass airstrip next to the Haddam Opera House Restaurant in East Haddam, Connecticut, where I got good and smashed before I had to repeat the nightmare of the return trip.

It was two years before I told him I hated to fly, two years of flying with him every weekend to places as close as Provincetown on Cape Cod for dinner or to places as far away as Eleuthera Island in the Bahamas for a long weekend.

"Why don't you go by yourself?" I suggested one Saturday as he collected his flight book and charts before leaving for the airport. I'll never forget the expression of surprise on his face.

"But you love to fly," he said.

"Actually," I said, taking a deep breath to give myself the courage to be honest, "I don't."

An argument ensued, the first of many over my aversion to flying, which would only strengthen over the next two years. More and more we went our separate ways; he into the air, as well as into the arms of other women, and me into the arms of alcohol.

It wasn't until I was in my forties, when my panic attacks started to diminish and eventually stopped, that I understood what a hell I'd been living in for the previous twenty years. Profound chronic anxiety had utterly controlled my life, and the need to keep it a secret because of the great shame I felt about it exacerbated an already deep sense of alienation that lingered from a parentless, displaced childhood.

It is sad to realize how unforgiving I was about my own emotions. Instead of vigorously and truthfully seeking help, including appropriate medication, I'd viewed the panic attacks as proof that I was "bad" rather than ill. So for twenty years, I chose to strong-arm myself through each day, to keep my terrible flaw a secret. How did I teach? How did I sit across the table from someone and carry on a conversation through an anxiety attack? How did I drive a car, ski with friends, attend classes in graduate school, *fly every weekend,* prey to the self-destructive behaviors of smoking, drinking, and starving, which seemed to ameliorate the anxiety attacks temporarily but did nothing to stop them?

MUCH OF MY estrangement from Laura had come as a result of needing to distance myself from those painful, anxiety-filled years of living in Boston. I didn't realize how bad they had been until I was safe in my own house in

Olivebridge. When I started writing I was flooded with sorrow and rage, two feelings I had either ignored or didn't know I possessed. After almost never crying, I seemed to cry for ten years straight. With all the safety nets gone—cigarettes, wine, obsessive exercising, and starvation—there was nothing left but to feel my feelings. And as bad and as frightening as that was, it wasn't until all my self-destructive behaviors stopped that I finally began to heal. Therapy helped, being with my horses and dogs helped, the solitude and beauty of my farm helped, but what helped the most was expressing it all in writing, finding a way to say in a story what I had been unable to express in real life.

Stephen King once said he never needed a therapist because he wrote books instead. I understand. Besides being a craft, writing is about discovering the truth. Whether it's fiction or nonfiction, the truth is what distinguishes good writing from bad. It is at the heart of any story. It is what the protagonist seeks, what the antagonist resists, and, ultimately, it is what the reader expects to find. False lines in a book, lines written to impress rather than to *express,* stand out like neon lights, and if there are enough of them, they ruin the book. The same is true in life. As long as I denied my own grief and rage—the truth at the center of my emotional experience—my life remained a bad book. Writing led me to acknowledge the truth of how I felt and, in doing so, ended the panic attacks.

It was hard to imagine explaining to Laura, who as a young adult always tried to include me, that living with her family had been very hard for me. No matter what her parents did, I had felt my separateness acutely. All three daughters bore a striking resemblance to their father as well as to all six of their paternal cousins. Every family get-together—and they were frequent—there were the tall, slim, blond cookie-cutter cousins, the boys incredibly handsome, the girls beautiful, all with the easy confidence of children who are rich and well loved. Then there were my uncle and his two brothers, three famously handsome Harvard men, Boston socialites, who, if they noticed me at all, referred to me as my aunt's niece.

This was not a family that lingered over feelings. I doubt any of the children heard "I love you" very often, if at all. I doubt there was much hugging. Certainly, I was never the recipient of any affection. My aunt and uncle were two of the most reserved people I have ever met. The one strong feeling my aunt had no trouble expressing was her dislike of her brother, my father. Everything about him embarrassed her: his drinking, his lowbrow sense of humor, his complete abdication of any responsibility, including for the raising of his two children. Who could blame her? But as a child, and even into adulthood, I wondered how much of her anger toward her brother was redirected toward me, the daughter who looked so much like him. My aunt's sense of duty had overcome whatever else she might have felt about taking me in, but I always felt her ambivalence.

Going back to Boston to spend time with Laura, her sisters, parents, or any of her cousins would always in some way mean going back to being the outsider. Just as Laura would always be the middle child in her family, I would always be the unwanted child. It was a feeling I had never completely overcome. In 1995, when writing began to flush out all the emotions I had suppressed about my childhood, I had to distance myself from that past. In Olivebridge, I established a family of friends, a close circle of people in which I never felt like the outsider. No one there had any connection to my past, an extraordinarily freeing fact for someone with my background. I wasn't the drunk's daughter, a burden to my aunt and uncle or any of the other relatives who took me in at different times. I wasn't a victim. In Olivebridge, for the first time in my life, I felt like I was on an equal footing with the rest of the world. I was in control of me.

Getting together with Laura that night meant not only stepping into the past, but also facing her hurt and anger at my distancing myself from her. I had never adequately explained to her my need to do this, partly because for years I hadn't understood it myself and partly because, when I did, the damage our relationship had already suffered seemed irreparable. I even wondered if she was coming to my first reading in the Boston area out of a sense of duty, like her mother, or whether she really wanted to see me.

At the hotel, I had just changed into one of the clean linen shirts when the phone rang. Laura was calling from the lobby. I told her to come up, nervous about what I would say, how much or how little to explain. The e-mail exchange that had set up our meeting had included her news about a new romance.

When she arrived we hugged, and she flopped onto the bed, tired from the long drive through heavy traffic. She said something nice about the book, adding incredulously, "*You're on a book tour.*"

I giggled. I felt amazed, too.

"*And you're in love,*" I said, equally incredulously. Laura's e-mail had also disclosed the fact that she hadn't dated for more than twelve years and hadn't been in love since college.

"Since you brought it up," she said, reaching for her pocketbook and pulling out an envelope of photographs, "I just happen to have some pictures."

She told me his name; I could see that he was teddy-bear handsome. They'd met on the job at an English as a Second Language program. In the pictures of them together, they looked utterly joyous.

It became clear to me that this was not the time to try to explain why we had become estranged. What was important was to listen to her. Then I told her about meeting Dennis Stock again, about how I felt as if I were at the edge of a precipice. It was as if we were two young women again, talking about boys.

We walked to the bookstore still talking about boys. We arrived only a few minutes early but it was empty except for the owner. She was flustered and contrite. She couldn't understand. She had advertised the reading for weeks, posted it on her web site, called many of her regular customers on the phone, and still, the store was empty. We stood surrounded by fifteen empty chairs and stacks of my books.

Miraculously, three women strolled in. They hadn't known there was a reading that night until one of them saw the notice in the newspaper. They had read the book and decided to come. Then a man entered. The owner of the bookstore knew him. He worked next door. So, counting my cousin and the owner, six people listened to me read. I reminded myself to read slowly, to take deep breaths, to just do it.

When I finished they asked questions. "Do you think you

were the only one who suffered as a child?" one woman asked.

I was mortified. She sounded accusatory, as though in writing a memoir I had whined about the same things others had borne silently, stoically, better. It was the very question I'd often asked myself, even as a child. What right had I to complain? And yet I had written a book in which I dared to complain, and in doing so had invited the very label I had dreaded the most, which this woman's question suggested: the poor little rich girl. Or was I hearing it wrong? "Suffering can be an isolating experience," I replied, "but I never felt I was the only one who suffered."

When it was over, when everyone had said what they needed to say, they thanked me and left. The owner was still apologetic. "It's one of the best books I've ever read," she insisted softly, barely able to look at me as I thanked her and said good night.

Laura and I headed for a restaurant. Now that the reading was over and the worst of my fears about no one—or hardly anyone—showing up had been realized but overcome I could begin to unwind. And even with all the years of unexplored silence still hanging between us, Laura and I had a pretty good time.

"I'm really glad you came," I said later as she got into her car.

"I wouldn't have missed it for anything," she said. "I'll see you again at your reading next week in Weston. A lot of people have told me they're coming. It won't be like tonight."

Standing next to Laura's car, it was impossible not to acknowledge the strong connection I felt to her, a woman I've known and loved since she was a baby, who shared the distinction of being the descendant of one of the scariest grandmothers ever, the grandmother who had become my legal guardian and who, over the years, we had often found much to laugh about.

This is what family *feels* like, I told myself. The good and the bad, the sad and the funny. *Stop wallowing in ancient history.*

"I love you," I told Laura. Awkwardly. Sincerely.

"I love you, too," she answered.

I HAD AGREED TO zigzag across New England, first driving two hours west to Edwards Books in Springfield, Massachusetts, for a 1:00 p.m. reading and then two hours southeast to Providence, Rhode Island, for a 7:00 p.m. reading at Books on the Square. There I had arranged to meet two friends from high school whom I hadn't seen in thirty years. On top of that, the night before, when I returned to the hotel after dinner with Laura, I had learned that a friend's thirty-four-year-old daughter had died. A few years earlier, her other child, a son in his twenties, had passed away suddenly. I decided to go home to attend the memorial service, which would be held in a few days, before going on with my tour.

All day as I drove, I thought of my friend and wondered how she could possibly bear the loss of her children. I was reminded of my depression after the death of each of my horses. The worst period of grief had followed the death of my Morgan mare, Georgia. Remembering that was as close as I could come to imagining how despondent my friend must be. I don't know if it's fair to compare the loss of a child to the loss of a beloved animal. I always feel guilty when I do it and yet, not having had human children, it is the only way I know of imagining the broken heart of a mother. I know that what I felt for Georgia was a deep and abiding love.

* * *

GEORGIA HAD BEEN my own choice. I'd picked her out after viewing countless mares on countless farms, and it was love at first sight. I'd bought her after realizing that I was forever out of love with my husband, and that it was only a matter of time until our divorce.

Georgia's first winter in my new home in Olivebridge followed a whole year of separation before she was returned to me following a custody battle with my now ex-husband. At first I thought her strange demeanor was related to being in a new barn with new stablemates, my two geldings, Tempo and Hotshot. She was a moody mare and I thought she was having adjustment problems. During the year I'd spent trying to get her back, I hadn't known where she was. I still didn't know. The court had ordered my ex to return her but he'd never said where he'd kept her all that time. I even wondered if she'd been abused.

All winter I sensed that something was wrong but it was hard to put my finger on what was different about her. Then one morning my alarm peaked. "Can you come right away?" I sniffled on the phone to the vet, wiping big tears off my face with the back of my hand. "I think it's cancer."

I hung up and stared through the window at my beautiful chestnut Georgia, grazing in the backyard. I'd let her out of the pasture to feast on the lawn because what did it matter if it was too rich and she got fat? What did it matter if she trampled the just-blooming daffodils? Georgia was only six years old and dying, so what did anything matter?

"She looks lumpy," I told a friend over the phone.

"Lumpy?"

"Or her legs are skinnier," I said, trying to articulate the

fact that her proportions had changed. She looked completely different. She was acting funny, too. But the word
that came to mind seemed too strange to say out loud.
"Desperate," I wanted to say. "She seems desperate." One day
during a snowstorm I had found her outside, not snuggled
down in her dry stall eating fragrant hay laced with her
favorite grasses, timothy and clover, but standing outside in
the wind, her mane and forelock whipping around her face
and neck, wet and tangled with little chunks of ice as she
tried to eat the bark of a tree growing just out of reach on
the other side of the rock wall. As I got closer I'd called her
name. She had turned to look at me with real fear in her
eyes. It made my heart jump. Georgia had never been afraid
of anything, certainly never of me. And I knew it wasn't me
she was afraid of now, but the trouble was, I didn't know
why she seemed frightened. I didn't know why she was trying to eat bark instead of hay and I didn't know why she had
chosen to leave her dry stall to stand outside in a blizzard.

But that morning it had all become clear when I had discovered the cancer and realized she was dying. I had found it
when I was brushing her belly and my hand had suddenly
bumped into a hard mass. I couldn't believe what I'd felt and
had bent down to look and there were her teats, usually soft
and droopy, now hard as rocks. My breath caught in my
throat as I had backed away from her in horror.

It was the first time I'd telephoned the vet since moving
to the area, so when Dr. Goodenow arrived, we introduced
ourselves as we stood next to his truck before I went to get
Georgia. He seemed like a gentle person but when I led
Georgia out of the barn, I could tell instantly she didn't like
him. She danced at the end of the lead line and trembled as

soon as his hand touched her neck. She looked at him sideways with a wild eye, emitting a continuous series of throaty grunts. She wanted nothing to do with this man. I was embarrassed by her reaction because he seemed so nice but it was obvious to us both that my horse didn't like him.

"I'm sorry," I said as she yanked herself away from his touch. "She's been acting weird for months."

It became impossible for him to examine her. She reared, she bit, she kicked, she got hysterical. He couldn't get within two feet of her.

"I'm going to have to twitch her," he said apologetically.

I hated twitching a horse. A twitch is a device vets used to control a horse who can't be controlled in any other way. The instrument is placed on the upper lip, pinching and twisting it to cause enough pain to stop a horse dead in its tracks. Most horses stood absolutely still under a twitch. And as soon as he put it on Georgia, she did, too.

I felt so guilty about allowing her to be twitched that I couldn't look at her. I was sure she was going to hate me for the rest of her short life, that I had irrevocably lost her trust. As I wallowed in guilt, Dr. Goodenow examined her.

"It's there," I said, waving my hand in the direction of the growth under her belly. "It's horrible," I added, in case he needed details.

He bent down to look under her belly, nodding when he saw it. "So that's the horrible mass," he said, as he felt around with his hand.

A few minutes later, with Georgia still twitched and immobile, he walked over to the back of his truck and pulled out two long, clear rubber gloves.

"Put this on," he said, handing me one. He slipped another

onto his own arm. It covered him all the way to the shoulder and so did mine. "I'll go first and then you can go," he said.

For a second I had no idea what he was talking about. He walked around to Georgia's tail, squeezed lubricant out of a tube, and smeared it all over his gloved arm. When he was done, he threw the lubricant to me so I could do the same. *Pelvic cancer. He was going to make me feel pelvic cancer!*

A second later he eased his hand into Georgia, and pretty soon his whole arm was inside her, right up to his shoulder. Georgia looked quietly terrified.

"Uh-huh," he said, feeling around, confirming what he already knew. "Good position," he mumbled, followed by a longish silence and then suddenly, "Teeth!"

Teeth? Tumors had teeth?

He withdrew his arm slowly and looked at me with a funny smile.

"That's a foal in there, not a tumor," he said. "She's ready to give birth at any time."

"Excuse me," I said to this poor vet, who obviously didn't have a brain in his head, "but she's never been bred."

The smile broadened across his face as he started smearing my gloved arm with lubricant. "Go ahead," he urged, "just follow the canal until you bump into something hard."

"I'm not really a medical buff. . . ." But he wasn't taking no for an answer and he started to guide my hand into the opening of the birth canal. I don't know why I was so scared but I was shaking and curious at the same time as my arm slipped deeper inside my poor twitched horse.

"OK," he said when he saw my arm couldn't go any further, "now move your hand around and see if you can identify anything."

Almost immediately I felt something hard. I let my fingers trace the outline. And then I traced it again. "A hoof!" I said, incredulous. I was feeling a tiny hoof.

"That's right," he encouraged. "Anything else?"

I pushed my arm a little deeper and felt something else hard. Teeth. I had found those teeth. I couldn't believe it. How could this foal have possibly ended up inside my horse?

And then it dawned on me that Georgia wasn't dying. She didn't have cancer and even though I had no specific idea of how she had gotten pregnant, the more amazing news was that my beloved horse was going to live.

We untwitched her and I led her back to her stall and from that moment on, I read every book I could find about pregnant mares and foaling and how to raise a foal. I read about all the things I should have been doing all winter and hadn't because I hadn't known she was pregnant. I was furious with my ex-husband for not telling me that he'd had her bred so I could have cared for her properly. I was furious that my complete ignorance about equine pregnancy had kept me from seeing her symptoms for what they were. I had felt foolish when Dr. Goodenow had had to explain that her teats were rock hard because they were full of milk, not full of cancer.

I had to make up for all the things I hadn't done for her in the previous eleven months. I increased her grain, added a daily bran mash, gave her vitamins and supplements and doubled her hay allotment. I also lavished her with the kind of cloying love she had never liked but I couldn't help it. I wanted her to know how sorry I was, how I finally understood.

I separated her from Hotshot and Tempo, giving her the back pasture all to herself and sprucing up the turnout shed to act as a foaling pen and nursery. It was the Ritz of turnout sheds, ankle deep in cedar shavings with a new wind block halfway across the front and a grain creep for her new foal. She was all set. I spent hours with her each day and slept in the loft above the turnout shed at night, determined to witness the birth of her foal and to help her if necessary.

Two weeks after the vet had announced she was pregnant, I got out of my sleeping bag in the shed loft, and walked back to the house for a hot shower. It was a chilly May morning and snowflakes mingled with the raindrops. I rushed through my shower and as I was toweling off, I looked out the window toward the back pasture to check on Georgia and there was her foal, standing in the pouring rain and snow next to her mother.

I threw on some clothes and ran back to the pasture. I had hardly been gone. Georgia had waited until I'd left and then had birthed her foal in less than twenty minutes. As I entered the pasture, I saw the afterbirth floating in a shallow puddle right next to the gate. She had birthed her baby in a puddle. Why hadn't she sheltered in the shed? I approached Georgia and her bay-colored baby slowly. I had no idea how she would feel about letting me meet her foal so I gave her plenty of time to let me know. But the closer I got, the clearer it became that she didn't mind at all. From the first minutes she appeared to be a very relaxed mother. Maybe too relaxed. Why was she letting her baby stand out in the rain?

The foal was wet and wobbly but looked healthy and, of course, adorable. I peeked under its belly and discovered it was a filly, a little girl. She didn't like me getting too near and clung to her mother's flank on the side furthest away from me. I spoke to Georgia gently with my hand on her halter, telling her what a wonderful horse she was, what a wonderful mother, what a beautiful baby she'd had, the whole time slowly leading her back to the turnout shed. The foal followed and once they were both inside, I filled Georgia's bin with feed and scattered fresh hay to encourage her to stay inside.

It worked and I felt immensely better now that they were both out of the weather. Georgia's appetite was good and she tucked right into her grain. I watched the foal nurse for the first time and when she was done, she gave a big sigh and collapsed her long legs carefully, nestling herself into the cedar chips for a much-needed nap. It was such a precious moment, unforgettable in its simple, natural unfolding. I hadn't witnessed the birth but in the end, Georgia had done it her way, which was even better.

As I stood under the overhang of the turnout shed, listening to the rain pound on the roof and watching the snowflakes mingle with the rain across the pasture, I felt a deep sense of contentment. My horse was safe with her foal and now they would be dry and warm. And for the first time in my long life with horses, I would have the chance to pick a name. It seemed like a big responsibility, as important as any other that involved taking good care of a horse. Right there I started thinking about the possibilities. In less than five minutes, I knew I had her name. It came to me just like that. I thought of all I'd been through in leaving my marriage and divorcing a man who didn't want to make it easy. I thought of how mean it had been for him to take Georgia and hide her from me, especially when he didn't care about her at all. I thought about the foal, how sweet and vulnerable she looked lying in the cedar chips with her long legs spread out in front of her like that. And there was her name, as clear as a nameplate tacked onto her stall door: I would call this amazing, accidental baby Sweet Revenge.

THE MORNING AFTER Georgia died I woke up and I didn't know who I was. During the twenty years she'd lived under my care, I was unaware of how much she had slowly become the defining symbol of my identity, of what my life represented. If I had to name just one thing, one essential truth about myself, to this day, it would be Georgia. She was, and remains still, the great love of my life. Not that she reciprocated it, but that never mattered to me. It was enough that I loved her, that her enormous, often difficult personality filled my heart every time I looked at her.

It was impossible for me to feel depressed in her presence. For one thing, she was gorgeous, and for another, she demanded so much of my attention that there was none left over for myself. Sometimes it was just a question of surviving her antics, but most often I'd had the great privilege of being swept into the joy of life this animal expressed with such unrestrained vigor.

She was three when she bucked herself into my heart, a not-too-promising youngster living among much bigger stars on a down-at-the-heels Morgan breeding farm in western New York. Her bad behavior barely registered compared to the instant recognition I felt at seeing *my horse,* the being with whom I was certain I would share the next forty years of my life.

For twenty years she had been the beginning and ending of every day, the perfect antidote to a bad childhood, a bad day, worries about the future. I'd counted on Georgia to be there into old age, mine and hers. And then she'd gotten sick, twenty years too early. Many horses live forty years or longer. Tempo and Hotshot had, but Georgia died when she was just twenty-three, and I was nowhere near ready.

The night before she died, I sat on the floor of her stall with my back against the wall and held her head in my lap. I never closed my eyes and neither did she. Even with an over-dose of bute for pain, her breathing was labored and there were sweat marks down her withers. I was glad it was a cool night and I could open her stall door to the outside, where we could look across the pasture and into the cloudless night sky filled with stars. She had been sick for a year with lamini-tis, a disease of the hoof that makes walking painful. When unresponsive to treatment, it eventually makes walking impossible. She would be euthanized in the morning, a deci-sion I had been unable to make without the gentle interven-tion of my one-time vet, Amy Grice, who for the past several years had practiced exclusively at the large breeding farms on the other side of the Hudson River. But prior to that, she had been the vet to all my horses for at least ten years.

Apparently, everyone had been telling me that Georgia wasn't going to make it: my farrier; Allie, who knew more about horses than anyone I knew; the vet I'd had for the past few years and liked very much; even a new farrier I'd called in to get a second opinion about the seriousness of Georgia's condition. All of them had said the same thing for months: she was terminal. But I'd never heard it. The closest I had come to understanding that she was dying was when the new farrier came, the one I had called for a second opinion. He was a man so respected and in such demand in the area that he hadn't accepted a new client in ten years. His coming at all was the first indication to me that something was very wrong, but it

was when he was done and didn't give me a bill that my denial
about her chances of survival first began to crack.

A few days after I consulted that second farrier, I saw Dr.
Grice's truck pull into my pasture. I hadn't seen her in a few
years, and I couldn't imagine why she had come. She was
already out of her truck and in the barn by the time I pulled
on my boots and walked across the pasture to join her. I
found her in Georgia's stall, a stethoscope around her neck,
listening to Georgia's heart. I waited until she was done and
then, with her hand still caressing the beautiful neck beside
her, she dropped the end of the stethoscope and looked at
me. Before she'd said a word, I'd understood. They had sent
her. My current vet, Allie, the farrier—I didn't know which
one but I knew someone had sent her to tell me what they
had all been trying to tell me for months.

Dr. Grice euthanized her the next morning. Allie was
with us and when it was over, Allie took me somewhere for
the day but I don't remember where. It was the following
morning that I woke up not knowing who I was. It wasn't
just that I had been riding and taking care of Georgia every
day for twenty years. It wasn't just that I loved her deeply. As
her illness had progressed, I had spent more and more time
nursing her and, in the last three months of her life, I had
been in the barn with her every three hours around the
clock. For a year, nothing had been more important to me
than saving Georgia's life. To say I tried everything is an
understatement. There is no cure for laminitis, only drugs
and various treatments to ameliorate pain and swelling with
the hope that, over time, the condition will resolve itself.
Georgia had had laminitis before and had always recovered,
but not this time.

She was the last of my four horses to die. First had been Lay Me Down, then, well into their forties, Tempo, and a few months later, Hotshot. After the death of Hotshot, Allie had given me a Haflinger gelding named Willie so Georgia wouldn't be alone in the barn. But with Georgia's death Willie was now alone in the barn. I didn't have the heart to get a new horse so two days later I gave Willie to a neighboring farm that already had two Haflingers.

After Georgia died, I wanted to burn down the barn. I couldn't bear to go in it. I couldn't even bear to look at it. I called Allie and told her she could take anything she wanted except Georgia's bridle and saddle. I helped her carry out halters, tack, feed buckets, blankets, unused meds, fly spray, and twenty years' worth of miscellaneous horse stuff including a spare paddock gate and a watering trough. We even unbolted the iron bars from the stall windows so she could use them in the new addition she was putting on her own barn.

The day we emptied my barn, I saw my horses walking in and out of their stalls all day. I heard Tempo pound on the wall with his front hoof the way he did every single morning and evening feed. I saw Lay Me Down in her blue New Zealand blanket, rushing in her choppy, arthritic gait to greet me with a misting sigh. I saw Hotshot, always near Lay Me Down, standing with his neck stretched over her stall door. I saw Georgia, not as she was when she was sick and could hardly walk, but trotting up and down the center aisle of the barn, pinning her ears at Lay Me Down whenever she passed her stall, nipping Hotshot because she could get away with it, and crushing me into a corner until I produced a treat. All day I watched them, their shadows flickering against the walls.

I felt robbed by Georgia's death, cheated out of the next twenty years that should have belonged to me. In the days following, I think my anger kept me sane. I hated the barn. I hated my house, the land, the pond. I hated anything connected to her. In the house I put away all her photographs. I took down the two paintings of her that I had commissioned. I changed my mind about keeping her bridle and gave it away. I kept her saddle but put it in the basement where I would never have to see it. At night I lay in bed and planned to tear down the fences and burn down the barn.

In the morning without horses to feed, I didn't know what to do with myself. The same feeling would return at the end of the day. In between, when, occasionally, people I didn't know asked what I did, I'd say, *Well, I used to have four horses.*

"Think of all the money you were spending on vets," my brother said one day as a way to try to comfort me, as a way to try to snap me out of my protracted grief.

"She was the same age as your daughter," I said and hung up on him.

For a year I didn't go near the barn and avoided looking at it, which wasn't easy since every window in my house but one faces it directly. It was 2002, the same year my relationship with Paul ended. I was writing books I couldn't sell, making too little money as a writing adjunct, and just beginning menopause. For all those reasons, but mostly because of the loss of Georgia, I didn't know who I was or what would become of me.

"I have this friend moving here from Texas," Allie said on the phone after Georgia had been dead a year. "She has two Thoroughbreds and needs a place to keep them."

I didn't know what to say. I hated horses.

"Look," she said into the silence, "I think it's time."

And so one morning, Rip and Sky arrived, two leggy Thoroughbreds, trailered all the way from Texas in a large horse transporter filled with other horses who were being delivered to various farms all over New England. Two cowboys in alligator boots and Stetson hats led them across my lawn to the pasture gate, where, after unhooking their lead lines, we stood and watched the horses as they cantered through the overgrown field on legs still stiff from their three-day journey across America. And, just like that, horses were back in my life. Beginning that day, I started to remember who I was. I e-mailed my brother to tell him.

> I finally understand who I am, what my purpose in life really is. I have been put here to take care of horses. I am someone who is meant to love horses.

On my way home I recalled that I had been grateful to Allie. That confirmed my decision to attend my friend's daughter's funeral. At the memorial service I gathered with a hundred or so others to celebrate the short life of a beautiful young woman I had never met. Looking at photographs of her, some taken with her deceased brother as they laughed and clowned for the camera, it was hard to grasp that they were both dead. I was afraid to look at Donna's face, to see the depth of her anguish. During the service, Donna's partner of many years addressed that fear. "Don't be afraid to come and see us," she said. "Our door is open. And we need you."

I knew how true that was.

{ 8 }

*O*n the drive to Springfield I tried to imagine who would come to a book reading scheduled for the middle of the day. Since hardly anyone had come to the evening readings, it seemed entirely possible that not a single person would show up. I comforted myself by remembering a book reading I had gone to years earlier at Barnes & Noble in Poughkeepsie to hear Michael Korda read from his book *Country Matters.* I'd made a point of getting there early to get a good seat near the front. I had particularly liked one of his earlier books, a history of Simon & Schuster entitled *Another Life.* When I arrived, there were five women sitting dead center in the first row of the fifty or sixty folding chairs that had been set up on the second floor. I settled near them and waited for the crowd to arrive. By fifteen minutes past the scheduled reading time, only four more people had come. So Michael Korda, who, in my opinion, had written one of the best books of all time about the publishing industry, read for ten people that night. It would become my mantra the summer of my book tour, whenever I faced all those empty chairs: *if Michael Korda could only get ten . . .*

I arrived in Springfield two hours early. I found the bookstore first, in a multilevel shopping mall in the middle of the city. I left the car in a parking garage and decided to walk around outside until it was time to go to the reading at one. I quickly discovered that Springfield was in economic trouble as I passed empty storefronts and abandoned buildings. I walked up a hill toward trees and an open space that I hoped might be a public park. It was a museum complex with a large memorial area in the middle filled with bronze statues of Dr. Seuss characters. I found a shady bench and watched a hundred or so elementary schoolchildren having a class picnic.

At twelve thirty I set out for the bookstore and on the way, *I had the book experience I'd waited for my whole life.* It was so momentous that I stopped in the middle of the crowded sidewalk and pulled out my notebook to record the time and date. On May 25, 2006, at exactly 12:51 p.m., I watched a perfect stranger walking on a city street in America *carrying my book.* I resisted the urge to run after her, calling, *Hey, I wrote that.* I resisted the urge to cheer.

A few minutes later, I walked into Edwards Books, still euphoric. I was greeted by the pretty owner, who extended her hand warmly and said, "You're an hour late. Everyone has left."

Suddenly I understood the expression on the face of the stranger hurrying past me, clutching my book. It wasn't the *Get out of my way, can't you see I have a good book to read* look I had imagined. No, what I had thought was the face of a determined reader was really the face of an angry one who had just been stood up by the author she went to the trouble of going to see on her lunch hour.

I stuttered an apology through a bad hot flash, dabbing at the sweat gathering at my temples with the sleeve of my linen shirt. Out of the corner of my eye I noticed a couple of dozen chairs set up in a semicircle in front of a big table with a display of my books at the back of the store. I fumbled through my purse for the reading schedule, for the piece of paper I carried with me everywhere, sure I could blame this terrible embarrassment on my publicist.

"Let's see," I said, squinting at the proof of my innocence, trying to read the tiny print without my glasses because I was too flustered to try to find them in the mess of my purse. But there it was, swimming up to me: twelve noon. The reading had always been scheduled for twelve noon.

"I don't know how I could have been so stupid," I said, stuffing the schedule back in my purse. But I did know because it wasn't the first time anxiety had caused me to make a dumb mistake. Still, I'd had the book-tour schedule for weeks. I didn't understand how I could have looked at "twelve" and read it as "one."

I offered to come back, to reschedule a reading for absolutely anytime. The owner insisted it was OK. Mix-ups happened. I apologized one more time, renewed my offer to come back, which she politely declined, and then left, feeling terrible.

I remained plunged in a deep gloom on the two-hour drive to Providence. I alternated between worrying about how my friend was coping with the death of her daughter, remembering the death of Georgia, and feeling bad about showing up an hour late for the reading. On top of that, I was nervous about the reunion with my high-school friends.

After I'd spent eighth and ninth grade at Northampton School for Girls, both the school and my family thought it would be better for me to attend a less strict, coeducational prep school, so, beginning in tenth grade, I was sent to Kents

Hill School in Maine. Initially, I was devastated to be leaving Northampton, where I had felt so happy for two years. I remembered walking around Kents Hill on my first day, feeling that I would never adjust to this new place. And the idea of going to classes with boys threw me. I'd been attending all-girls schools since fifth grade.

But later on that first day at Kents Hill, I'd met Ellen, Sandy, and Nan and everything had changed. The four of us had crowded into Ellen's small dorm room to sit around and talk. What initially brought us together was the coincidence that Ellen, Sandy, and I were all originally from Rye, New York. Sandy and Ellen knew each other from having attended the same public high school the year before. Nan was just friendly and audacious enough to walk into a room with three strangers and introduce herself before flopping down on the bed to join in the conversation. The closeness the four of us developed that day lasted for the next three years and beyond.

I was the only one who had lost touch with the other three for the past thirty years. This had nothing to do with loving them any less and everything to do with my growing feelings of inadequacy and shame at the panic attacks and drinking that slowly began to take over my life not long after I'd graduated from Kents Hill. As long as I lived in the protective, familial environment of a small prep school, where I felt like a loved and valued member of the community, I was fine. But as graduation approached, I did not share my classmates' enthusiasm about escaping the strict, regimented days of prep-school life for the heady freedom of college. The more excited Nan, Sandy, and Ellen became about going off to college, the more ashamed I became for feeling just the opposite. There was nothing I dreaded more than graduating.

I watched Ellen, Sandy, and Nan grow up during those last months at Kents Hill at the same time I saw myself regress into a scared child. I was so ashamed of what was happening to me that telling them about it was out of the question. The closer we got to graduation day, the more distant from them I felt.

The summer after graduation another friend and I rented a room in an all-girls rooming house in Chatham on Cape Cod. On the surface, getting a job and spending the summer on the Cape was any teen's dream come true. It was swarming with college students working in restaurants and hotels and at other minimum-wage jobs just for the thrill of being there. But for me it wasn't an exciting taste of freedom; it was simply that I had nowhere else to go. At eighteen, I was officially homeless. There was no parental home to return to, no place I felt I had any right to be.

I was thirteen when I told the headmistress at Northampton School for Girls that I would kill myself if forced ever to return to my grandmother's house. I was terrified of her and her German chauffeur, Franz. Her crazy rules included forbidding my brother and me to talk to each other (on the rare occasions over the years when we were in her house at the same time), never being allowed to leave the house except with my grandmother, and not being allowed to have friends. The rules were endless, and since I was always in violation of at least one of them (eating too slowly, mumbling, not standing up straight, scuffing my heels, not putting something away right), I spent most of my days there restricted to my bedroom.

After my threat, the question of what to do with me during school vacations and summers became problematic. Often I spent time with my aunt and uncle outside of Boston, but I was also sent to summer schools, other relatives' homes, the houses of classmates, and, once, to France for the summer. But suddenly, at eighteen, I was supposed to make major decisions for myself. I had never had the freedom even to choose what I ate, and now I had to decide where I would live and how I would support myself. What should have been a summer of revelry enjoyed with the rest of my peers was a time of unmitigated anxiety about facing the world alone. I wasn't ready. I was eighteen going on ten. I still longed for a mother and father or a school full of nurturing teacher-parent surrogates. I knew how strange I had become that summer when, after speaking to Nan on the phone, I heard her whisper, as she passed the phone to Ellen, "She's getting so *weird.*"

I knew I was weird, but not until Nan's whispered remark did I realize others could see it, too. In that moment I understood I had lost my three closest friends. They had gone somewhere I couldn't follow and, worst of all, they knew it. Over the next year, I saw the three of them twice more, but each time was so stressful for me, as I attempted to keep up appearances, that when I left to attend the University of Colorado, I didn't tell them and left no forwarding address. They continued to get together every few years, unsuccessfully trying to find me each time they met. It wasn't until I sent the postcard announcing the publication of my book to an old address I had for Ellen that we reconnected.

On the way to Providence I wondered what I would say to Ellen and Nan (Sandy couldn't make it), whether there would be a moment that night or the next day when we would talk with the same candor we'd shared in high school, when I'd be able to tell them anything. I wondered if that feeling would ever come back. Ellen, Nan, and Sandy had children, husbands, solid careers, achievements the world recognizes as legitimate. Until publishing a book, my biggest achievements had been nothing I could casually mention with pride at a dinner party: I stopped drinking! I stopped starving! I stopped panicking! On a psych unit I was an overachiever; in the real world I was a *very* late bloomer.

Between roads closed for construction, rush-hour traffic, and stupid mistakes, I spent an hour driving around Providence before finding my hotel. I was a wreck when I dragged my suitcase across the lobby at five o'clock. I'd have about two hours to shower and rest before meeting Nan and Ellen in the lobby to go to the seven o'clock reading. I checked in and a few minutes later walked into the corner room on the top floor overlooking the harbor. With every accommodation in Providence full because of graduations, somehow Kathy had managed not only to book the best room in the hotel for me, but the best room in Providence. I felt absurdly pampered.

I returned to my car for something and as I was walking through the lobby again I noticed a tall thin woman wearing a jean jacket and a long summery skirt standing at the registration desk. We turned to look at each other at the same time and I recognized Ellen, the girl voted best looking by the 1968 graduating class of Kents Hill School. I couldn't believe how beautiful she still was and how *thin*.

"Susan Richards." She smiled, gliding across the lobby. "I've been trying to find you for thirty years."

"God, you're gorgeous," I said, and we hugged hard.

"Look who I found," Ellen said over my shoulder. I turned and there was Nan, walking through the front door.

"Jesus," she said, "where the *hell* have you been hiding all these years?"

Nan always had an edge, a kind of in-your-face toughness that in high school had been appealing but later came to intimidate me. In tenth grade, the boys at Kents Hill didn't think Nan was much to look at but by twelfth grade, she was the girlfriend of the best-looking guy in school.

My plans for taking a shower and relaxing were suddenly changed. Ellen wanted to go to the Salvation Army store near the hotel, famous for being one of the biggest on the East Coast, and also to a music store in search of the kind of CDs she can't find in the rural Maine town where she lives. I'd been on the road since nine o'clock that morning and desperately needed some downtime alone in my room. I still felt awful about my screwup at the bookstore in Springfield but I heard myself agreeing to join them on this shopping trip.

As we climbed into Nan's car, thirty-eight years evaporated. We were the same three girls who had once talked endlessly in each other's rooms. We finished each other's sentences, rudely interrupting, and laughed easily and often. I discovered that we were all in the helping professions: Ellen was a social worker and Nan, a nurse. After the Salvation Army store, we went to the music place.

THE TRUTH IS I hardly ever listen to music. It isn't that I don't like it, it's just that I have fallen in love with silence. It happened when I moved to Olivebridge and for the first time in my life lived alone in my own house. It was December, before the first snowfall, and I stood in the empty living room with the real estate agent next to me and looked out at the fields and the pond, awash in silence and sun. I knew I had to live there. I had to live *in* that silence. It seemed like a miracle that any place could be that quiet, that peaceful. I used to say I bought the house for the pond, for my Newfoundland, Bear, who loved to swim. And though there was much truth in that, it was the silence, the absence of human voices, that I needed.

I credit the house for helping me to stop drinking. The only thing I remember clearly about that first year of being sober is sitting in a chair in the living room, alternating between staring at the pond and rereading all of Jane Austen. I know I must have done other things but nothing else is as clear to me. Watching the pond change through the seasons was like watching a slow, beautiful story unfold, a story with a plot and a pace equal to what was unfolding inside me as I emerged from alcoholism. And Jane Austen? Maybe I needed to be in a world where, in the end, strong young women prevailed. Maybe I needed to know a happy ending was possible.

ONCE, EARLY IN my sobriety, on a hot night in the middle of July when I couldn't sleep, I got up and went with my Newfoundland and a rubber inner tube down to the pond. The peepers were at their summer loudest, a chorus of thousands trilling into the soupy air as I climbed into the tube to sit with my legs dangling over the side into the warm water. Whatever had been troubling me that night vanished and, floating on the still surface, I experienced the most profound sense of peace I'd ever known. Just before dawn I fell asleep, still floating in the inner tube with my Newfoundland's great head and shoulders flopped across my chest.

Fields, water, animals: these are the things that helped me. People came later. First, I had to get away. I had to find a place in which to silence the past, to silence the voices. For a while, any human voice seemed too reminiscent of the ones that had been so hurtful. I think at the beginning of my sobriety if I could have figured out a way to avoid humans completely I would have. Alcoholics Anonymous calls that "isolating" and cautions the newly sober to avoid it. This was one of the few suggestions from AA that I ignored. I spent as much time alone as I possibly could. To this day, twenty-four years later, I relish my snatches of solitude. They are less frequent now, but always restorative.

I still love silence. It is as necessary to me for writing as my computer. I get up at five because it is the most silent part of the day. In the winter, five in the morning isn't just silent, it's *still,* an even more exquisite form of silence. A lot can happen in stillness. It's the most naturally healing element in the world.

This love I have of silence, of stillness, can be a difficult thing to explain. I almost got into an argument once when a friend suggested I buy wind chimes as a gift for another friend.

"*Wind chimes?*" I gasped as though she had suggested subwoofers for the kitchen.

"Actually, they produce harmonic healing," she said, sounding a little condescending.

"What about listening to the *leaves and the birds?*"

"OK, OK," she mumbled, "but most people think wind chimes are nice."

And that's what bothered me—that most people thought wind chimes were nice, that *tinkling* was better than silence, that *tinkling* was better than leaves rustling or birds singing or tree frogs peeping or cicadas vibrating in the August heat or crows cawing at each other in the pasture. It wasn't just the silence wind chimes destroyed; they blocked every sound in nature.

But I'm self-conscious because I don't know more about music. It's like television, a whole world I don't know. I was rarely allowed to watch TV as a child—only the news with David Brinkley and Chet Huntley, sitting up straight (no slouching!) next to my grandmother on the couch after dinner. My aunt and uncle in Weston didn't buy a television until all three daughters were safely away in college, and televisions didn't exist at prep school.

It took airplanes flying into the World Trade Center for me to go out and buy my first television. The morning of the tragedy I was driving back from the grocery store, listening to the horror unfold on National Public Radio, when about four miles from my home I passed a house with the front door wide open and the television clearly visible and turned on in the living room. I pulled into the driveway and walked through the front door. The owner of the house was sitting on the couch, and he barely acknowledged me when I introduced myself and sat down. For the next two hours, though complete strangers, we cried and talked together, stunned by what we were watching.

Later, at home listening to the news on NPR, for the first time radio seemed inadequate. The world had changed that morning. The horror had gotten much closer. I bought a television a few days later and had a satellite dish installed.

Overnight I went from no channels to 507. For a few months I rushed home after work to gorge on whatever program I found. It was like living in a cineplex. I bought microwave popcorn, and after dinner, instead of taking the dogs for a walk or reading or correcting essays, I'd head up to the bedroom and, with the dogs clumped around me on the bed, I'd click through the 507 channels, equally fascinated by the dreadful and the wonderful.

The love affair didn't last long. Maybe television came too late in my life and at fifty-one, my DNA was permanently altered to favor radio. I missed NPR with its less sensationalized, less manipulative, less intrusive voice. Maybe the same thing has happened with music, and my DNA has changed to favor silence.

AT SIX O'CLOCK Nan suggested we go to a new wine bar right around the corner from the bookstore. Her son and his girlfriend, who couldn't attend the reading, might stop in to say hello. With that, the last hope for a shower and a change into fresh clothes disappeared for good. Yet I had a real desire to meet Nan's son. It was as hard to imagine her as a mother as it was as a nurse. It was easier to imagine the three of us sneaking food out of the dorm kitchen in the middle of the night than doing anything as grown-up as bearing children or running a community health clinic.

Fifteen minutes later we were sitting on tall stools around a small table in a noisy, upscale wine bar. Nan and Ellen were drinking white wine, and I was drinking seltzer. It was the first time since meeting at the hotel that we'd actually sat down face to face to talk. So far I knew very little about their lives of the past thirty years, and they knew little more about mine.

As we struggled to hear each other over the din of voices echoing off the marble floor and glass walls, I was sad that I had cut them out of my life for so long. It had taken me thirty years to risk seeking them out, to risk being as bold as Nan, to show up again as if I belonged. If it hadn't been for the book, would I have tried to find them? Would I have dared? The truth is, the negative voices from my childhood did such a thorough job that I doubt I'll ever be able to silence them completely. I've talked to many people from similar backgrounds, people who have grown up unwanted and unloved on a steady diet of criticism. Among other things, we seem to share the idea that you are what you accomplish. It's not good enough just to be a decent person because being a decent person got you nowhere as a child. Or, as I've seen it expressed in writing about the nature of low self-esteem, many of us have become human *doings* instead of human beings.

Avoiding people, especially avoiding intimate relationships, is one way to turn down the volume on the self-hate tape. In living alone, there's no one around to remind you that you're subhuman. On the other hand, it's lonely and a significant chunk of yourself doesn't really believe the baloney about being no good and wants to join the herd.

When I used to imagine what it would be like to publish a book, beginning years before I'd ever written one, there were two fantasies. One was that the people who had hurt me would read it and be sorry (they weren't; by the time the book was out, the most egregious offenders were dead and, yes, this was a revenge fantasy), and the second was that the people I loved would read it and want to find me. One day I would answer a knock at the door and it would be an old friend I hadn't seen in twenty or thirty years and she would say, *Hey, I read your book and I just had to find you* and she would hand me a still-warm casserole and invite me to join her women's group. And just like that, publishing a book would end a life of isolation.

The desire for revenge left me years ago but the desire for a family never has. Although somehow acquiring close connections by publishing a book was indeed my wish, it was one I scarcely believed possible. A fantasy like that seemed on par with throwing a coin into a fountain and going home expecting to find the bag of money you wished for waiting by the door. But in a way, that's exactly what was happening as, one by one, relatives and close friends from the past reappeared.

I think the animal part of us is wise and intuitive, and twenty-four years ago, it had led me to an oasis of quiet beauty where, alone in my own house for the first time in my life, it was safe enough to wake up. It is no accident that four months after I moved to the farm in Olivebridge, I stopped drinking. It was the first step in the long process of loosening the grip of the past. I had no conscious awareness of this at the time. I just knew I needed to go far away from bad memories—of people, places, and things—and start over. It took a horse to teach me that living in quiet isolation for the rest of my life wasn't necessarily the best plan. It worked for a while, but Lay Me Down had seemed to tell me in her own way that the time would come for me to rejoin the herd. Not just the human herd, but my own herd, the very people from whom I had distanced myself.

To be honest, I was afraid to reconnect with my relatives, afraid that all these years later, I would still feel like the outcast, the rotten egg. But getting a book published had given me the confidence to risk it, and the book tour gave me a structure in which to do it. I could send a postcard announcing the book's publication. I could invite them to a reading. They might come. It could be a beginning.

A FEW MINUTES before seven, we walked around the corner to Books on the Square. The store was big, bright, cheerful . . . and empty.

"I didn't realize it was graduation weekend when I booked this reading," apologized the owner. "Usually we get a good crowd."

It was the third reading in a row that I'd been told a bigger crowd "usually" came and it was impossible not to believe it was the book's fault. I was embarrassed that Ellen and Nan were witnesses to this sign of the book's failure, my failure.

We waited until seven thirty, then sat in a small circle of couches set up near the big windows at the front of the store and I read for four people: Ellen, Nan, the owner, and one customer. It felt ridiculous. Outside people walked by, dressed up, on their way to graduation dinners all over town. Snatches of their chatter and laughter passed easily through the windows. *Michael Korda once read for ten,* I reminded myself.

Later, as we walked to dinner, Nan told me that sometimes the same thing happened to her husband, who is also a writer. Her words took the edge off the shame I felt.

After we'd been shouting bits of our life stories across the table to each other for an hour, Ellen leaned over and yelled into my ear, "What about men?" Ellen and Nan leaned so far forward to hear my answer that their heads almost touched in the middle of the table. I leaned forward, too, until it looked like we were talking into a mic hidden in the carna-tions. What would I say about Dennis Stock? I'd met him twenty-four years ago and thought he was profoundly arro-gant. Since then I'd seen him once for fifteen minutes and we'd exchanged two e-mails and now, whenever I thought of him, I felt this tug in my stomach as if I hadn't eaten for two days. Suddenly, I knew that I would have dinner with him on Tuesday night. Even though it might feel as if I were being dragged to a scary doctor's appointment, six nights from now I would sit across the dinner table from Dennis Stock and see what happened because I was *curious*. It was the one feeling I could name, express with confidence, say out loud, and know that it was true.

"I've met this guy," I said, "and I'm really curious about him."

WHENEVER I RETURN from a trip, I know how good the house sitter has been by the way the dogs greet me at the door. This time when I walked up the basement stairs from the garage and entered the living room, all three dogs stared at me from the couch without getting up. I stared back, wondering how long it would take before they realized the most important person in the world had just entered the room, the person, as I'd explained to my vet once, who would throw herself in front of a train to save them.

Luna blinked a few times and Noche yawned and stretched out his front legs as if considering getting up, but then thought better of it. Lucy lifted her head and looked at me and then gave her tail one hard *thwump* against the couch before going back to sleep.

"Hey!" I shouted at them, hurt and happy at the same time. They'd obviously had no trouble bonding with Kristen. I dropped my purse and collapsed to the floor.

"Somebody better get over here fast," I threatened. As soon as my knees touched the rug, all three of them flew off the couch and I was covered by twirling pugs and a gyrating Lab. I closed my eyes and groped at fur, feeling a tail, a wet nose, Luna's nipping teeth all over my hands. I squealed their names, and it made them crazier. The pugs twirled across the rug in one of their ferocious mock battles while Lucy's bull-whip tail beat me across the head and swept the coffee table clean of books and magazines and the same poor little candle she has swept off the table almost every day of her life. I don't know why I still keep it there except for the fun of watching how far she can launch it across the living room.

I get the same feeling every time I walk into my house for the first time after I've been gone for a few hours, a few days, or a few weeks. It's a feeling of utter gratitude for both the beauty of its setting and for whatever circumstances of fate have allowed me to live here. It is the one place on earth I feel safe and welcome. It is *home* in the most profound sense; the place I feel attached to the earth. I can't think of anything more beautiful than a hay field, and my house is surrounded by them, separated by stone walls farmers built over a hundred years ago. If I deserve this place at all, it is only because I love it so much.

SITTING IN ALMOST the exact center of the property is a small round pond, a magnet for all kinds of wildlife that once inspired a book I began that I called *A Year by the Pond*. But instead of a book, it turned into a journal I've been keeping since 1998. The first entry reads

June 29, 1998 5 p.m.

The pond is quiet. No green heron, no sign of the Hollywood-size, thundering-footstep snapping turtle. However, that turkey just ran down the gravel path on this side of the stone wall. He looked like the roadrunner. He's been hanging around for weeks, taking dirt baths in my

squash patch. Why? Prickly squash vines make good back
scrubbers? He flattened them last week so the next time
I saw him I chased him away. Where are the others? All
last fall the turkeys traveled in large packs. Herds? Flocks?
And now just this one. Maybe an adolescent male. Too
young for a wife and while the others are busy raising
young, he's free to wander. Lonely like me but living in this
paradise.

I was still living in this paradise, still lonely sometimes, still
watching the pond. One of my favorite sights was the flock
of wild pigeons that lived in the hayloft of my neighbor's
barn and flew over the pasture every morning and evening
for a drink. They would circle overhead once or twice before
landing on the near shore. I loved the predictability of their
arrival, their proprietary attitude toward this little body of
water. It was as much theirs as mine. I loved the flock's long
graceful swoop low across the pond's surface just before they
landed and walked—what else?—pigeon-toed to the water's
edge. When they were done, they lifted into the air as one,
and I would hear a swoosh as they flew over the house on
their way home.

I woke up Saturday morning in my own bed, surrounded
by my dogs and cat, enjoying the familiar sound of crows arguing in the pasture. I didn't really know if they were arguing,
but five or six of them stood in a circle with their necks
stretched forward and cawed at each other. It went on and
on. The guest room was the only room in the house that
didn't face this pasture, nonetheless, people who have spent
the night there have told me that the sound of these crows
in summer woke them up. Others have told me that the

peepers kept them awake, and still others that the silence was "peculiar." The sounds of crows and peepers and silence— they are not for everyone but are music to me.

IT WAS THE day I had decided I would call Dennis to accept his invitation to dinner on Tuesday night. The idea of talking to him unnerved me, but I couldn't put it off any longer. It felt like a big step, switching from e-mailing to talking. I lay in bed making up rules for how to—for once in my life—do this differently, for how to put dating on an equal footing with, say, going to the grocery store or shopping for shoes.

It's just a date, I told myself, *it's no big deal.*

That's a lie, said a little voice.

OK, dating will never be like trying on shoes. But he better like sleeping with dogs.

Whoa! said the little voice. *You're already sleeping with him? Maybe you better let me make up the rules.*

You're right, I really got ahead of myself.

OK, said the little voice. *There's only one rule: no matter what, be yourself.*

Right, I've gotten much better about that, don't you think?

Not with men, said the little voice. *You still tend to be too accommodating.*

OK, less accommodating. I'll really work on that.

If you can be more honest, everything else will take care of itself, pointed out the little voice.

I can't believe I'm fifty-six and still learning how to be myself around men.

SEVERAL YEARS AGO my friend Allie and I shared a house exchange in England for three weeks in the southwest county of Dorset, surely one of the most beautiful places on earth. We were standing in line in a bakery one morning in the little town of Wool, waiting to order our daily breakfast of tea, scones, and clotted cream when Allie, a most gregarious traveler, befriended Jeffrey, a fellow scone lover and eighty-year-old sheep farmer, who was standing in front of us in line. Charmed by Allie after only a brief chat, he invited us both to a garden party he and his wife were hosting at their house that very afternoon.

At two o'clock, we drove down Jeffrey's driveway, a beautifully preserved stretch of a two-thousand-year-old Roman road, and arrived at his four-hundred-year-old stone farmhouse. As we got out of the car, we were greeted by his frail but elegant-looking wife. It was the second week in August and as we followed her along a little gravel path to the back of the house, we soon found ourselves standing among twenty or thirty other guests in a large English garden in full bloom. It seemed to Allie and me to be the quintessential English experience, and we were speechless with the charm of it all. The lawn was thick and lush and emerald green, and it was surrounded by a maze of flower beds bursting with color and sweet aromas. There were little orchards of various fruit trees, a topiary garden, and best of all, tables set with white linen, silver, and china, covered with cakes, cookies, tarts, and, of course, pots of steaming tea.

After receiving a tour of the gardens and barn, where we watched the sheep being milked as Jeffrey explained how it was then processed into organic yogurt, Allie and I found ourselves back on the lawn, sitting on a bale of hay, talking to several other guests who were seated next to us in lawn chairs. We spent most of the afternoon chatting with

Charlotte, an interesting and friendly grande dame in her nineties, who spoke to us at length about England's efforts, as well as her own, to help preserve wildlife. Later we learned she was one of the richest women in England. There was no hint of this when we were talking to her except for the last thing she said to us as we were saying our goodbyes. I told her how lucky I felt to have met her since, except for Allie's friendliness, our meeting never would have happened because I was too shy to talk to strangers in line at a bakery.

She said she, too, had been horribly shy all her life, until now. Her biggest regret was that she had spent so much of her life trying to be what other people expected her to be, and it was only as she became an old woman that she had stopped *accommodating* others.

She had just described me and what I most disliked about myself. As Allie and I drove away that day I remember thinking, *I don't want to be ninety and still stifled by my need to please others.*

My friend Gretchen had recently told me that one of her goals as a teacher that semester was to let go of the need to be liked by her students. I was surprised that someone as independent minded as she was cared what anyone thought. But as soon as she said it, I decided to adopt her goal for myself, not just with students but with everyone.

The women I most admire are the ones who speak out. In graduate school, I befriended a woman named Jane, who, on the first day of a class called Group Dynamics, opened the assigned textbook and noticed the publication date was 1968. This was in 1988. She asked the professor to explain why we were using a twenty-year-old book in a relatively new area of psychology where emerging studies were adding important information all the time. I remember the anger in the professor's eyes when Jane didn't accept his explanation and insisted that a more up-to-date text be selected. It was a thrilling confrontation, and the class of twenty-two women listened wide-eyed as Jane delivered her ultimatum: assign a new text or she would take her complaint to the department chair. When a new textbook was assigned, I remember thinking that for many years the mostly female students had accepted the status quo before someone like Jane had come along to challenge it. Listening to Jane opened a door for me.

At fifty-six and poised on the threshold of a new adventure with Dennis Stock, it seemed like a good idea to banish my inner Charlotte and to call forth my inner Jane. I asked myself what would happen if, within reason and without being hurtful, I honestly said what I thought and felt without regard to how it would be received. What did I have to lose? Maybe nothing more than the wrong people cluttering up my life as I tried to pretzel myself into someone that someone else might like.

BEFORE CALLING DENNIS, I took my time feeding and brushing Chet, my boarder, luxuriating in the smells and sounds of the barn after a week of being away. Chet was a sweet but untrained and rambunctious three-year-old Appaloosa. My greatest contribution to her training had been to introduce her to dogs and peppermint candies. She preferred peppermints but enjoyed giving Lucy a good chase around the pasture when we arrived to do chores in the morning. If Lucy wasn't with me (a rare occurrence), then Chet tried to play with me in the same way, running at me full speed to get the chase going. She seemed surprised and disappointed when I didn't budge and instead flailed my arms at her and shouted, *No!* Once, after a rain when the grass was wet, she ran straight at me, locking her front legs just a few feet in front of me, attempting to go too quickly from a full gallop to a full stop. She slid into me, knocking me down, and fell on top of me. Luckily, it happened near the barn entrance, where it gets good and muddy after a hard rain, so there was enough give in the ground to cushion me, and I wasn't hurt.

Another morning I had just poured grain in her feed bin and was shutting her stall door, so she could eat without being distracted by Lucy, when she was spooked by a noise. The stall doors are heavy and hang on overhead tracks, clicking shut at the middle as well as at the bottom so a horse can't kick the door out. The door hadn't quite latched shut yet when Chet ran out of her stall, oblivious to the door in her way and me behind it. As she left the stall, she thrust the door up. It struck me full force, lifted me into the air, and flung me across the center aisle of the barn. My back slammed into the opposite wall and I slid to the floor like a rag doll. I sat on the cement with my legs splayed out in front of me for a few minutes, absorbing the shock, while I wondered how many bones were broken. Slowly, I got to my feet and walked around, testing ankles and knees and especially my chronically bad lower back to see if everything had survived the blow. I discovered that not only wasn't I hurt, but my back actually felt better than it had in months. Apparently getting slammed into a wall acted as some kind of super chiropractic adjustment.

Still, I was cautious around Chet in a way I never had been with my own horses, partly because she was young and

unpredictable and partly because I was older and more frag-
ile. But there was still nothing more pleasurable or thera-
peutic for me than being in the barn tending a horse. It
assuaged my anxieties about publishing, book readings,
reunions with family and old friends, and calling Dennis
Stock about getting together for dinner on Tuesday. At one
time I had thought of my barn as new but since the deaths of
my own horses, it had come to represent the passage of
time. Now I saw it as an old and poignant symbol of my earlier life. Being in my barn was to be in all the barns I'd spent
time in since I was a child, when they had been my refuge.

DESPITE MY RESOLVE, I went into a kind of emotional
blackout later when I called Dennis about dinner. There was
no sign of my inner Jane when I responded to his question
about where I'd like to eat. A*nywhere's great, I'm easy,* was what
I chirped. *Anywhere* is not great, and I'm not particularly easy
when it comes to food. I like good food. I don't mean that it
has to be expensive, I mean that I prefer organic or natural
foods. Why hadn't I suggested one of my favorite restaurants? I hung up hating myself. So far, nothing was different.
I was still running for Miss Nice USA

I liked Dennis's voice. It was low and growly and he
retained a New York accent on some words, like dog, which
he pronounced *dawg.* I don't remember when I started
thinking a New York accent was appealing. At one time it
would have made me cringe. Dennis also spoke slowly and
deliberately, choosing his words carefully, not because he
seemed to be nervous but because he seemed thoughtful.
Our conversation had his full attention. It did not have mine.
I was organizing the contents of my pocketbook while we

spoke, trying to distract myself from my anxiety over this upcoming date. We agreed to meet at his house at 6:00 p.m. on Tuesday.

Tuesday came and I was, predictably, a wreck. It was not just Dennis. Over the weekend two newspapers and a radio station had called to set up interviews and my agent phoned to say someone from Teri Hatcher's production company as well as an independent film company in New York City had expressed interest in optioning the film rights for the book. Helen told me that one of the partners in the independent film company was so moved by the book that she went to New Jersey the day after she finished reading it and adopted a horse from a rescue group. Selling the film rights was something I had never imagined.

I called Allie to ask who she wanted to play her in a possible film.

"Uma Thurman?" I suggested.

"No," said Allie, "I don't think so."

"I know. Gwyneth Paltrow would be perfect," I said.

"What about Renée Zellweger?" Allie asked. We started to laugh. It was all so preposterous. Neither of us believed for a second a movie about us would ever be made.

"Sandra Bullock for you," Allie said.

"Catherine Keener," I said.

Now every time we're together, no matter what we're talking about, one of us will suddenly say, "Cate Blanchett?" or maybe "Diane Lane?"

"For you?"

"No, for me."

* * *

AT SIX O'CLOCK that evening I pulled into Dennis's circular gravel driveway and was immediately reminded of a book I'd loved as a child. It featured a little house that sat in a field on the curve of the earth where a mother, father, sister, brother, and two grandparents lived. I loved that house; you could look into the front windows and see straight through to the fields on the other side. Dennis's house sits on the top of a grassy knoll surrounded by fields of wildflowers in bloom with a view of mountains in the distance. I could look through the windows on either side of his front door right through the house to the wildflowers and mountains on the other side. It was utterly charming.

As I parked, the front door opened and Dennis appeared. He waved from the top of the front steps. I got out of the car, suddenly not caring what happened that night. In the vernacular of my students, *Whatever*. I strolled up the flagstone path as if nothing in the world could be easier.

"Welcome to a mess," he said. His house was being painted. He was wearing khaki shorts with pockets everywhere and a short-sleeved blue denim shirt. He looked like a photographer on safari. Or maybe I was just remembering something I'd heard about him after I'd bought his house twenty-four years ago, that after moving to France, he'd gone off to photograph wildlife somewhere in Africa. He was tan and his prescription aviator-type glasses had turned dark on the still sunny evening. I liked his watch—a thick curved crystal, a black leather band. It could have been a Timex but it looked elegant. Everything about him seemed elegant. He moved carefully, deliberately, the same way he spoke. I got the feeling he never said or did anything he didn't mean.

Inside the house, the "mess" meant a dozen or so cardboard boxes stacked neatly in the living room, which was part of a large open-floor-plan area that included a kitchen and dining room, all facing a bank of floor-to-ceiling windows with a view of meadows and mountains. It was a bigger, more dramatic version of the house I had bought from him. The only thing missing was the pond.

The furnishings, the art, the colors—all of it was unusual and so lovely. Leaning against the wall in the entrance hall was a six-foot-tall wooden rack holding dozens of spools of colorful silk threads that he'd found at an old textile mill in France. On the opposite wall leaned a six-foot-tall, three-foot-wide antique wooden sleigh thresher. Hundreds of sharp stones stuck into grooves on the bottom helped to separate the wheat from the chaff as the heavy sleigh was dragged over wheat by mules. The house was filled with other French antiques—crude wooden work tables; a spinning wheel; large, colorful pottery—as well as Hopi and Zuni kachinas and Navaho rugs from the southwestern part of the United States. On many walls poster-size prints of some of Dennis's most famous photographs were displayed. Audrey Hepburn smiled from the window of her limousine, and James Dean walked through a rainy Times Square. There was a couple lying in the sand on a deserted California beach under the enormous shadow of an airplane wing, and then my favorite—the back of a young girl dancing alone on the stage at the Venice Rock Festival in front of thousands of spectators. There were also large color prints of flowers—gorgeous, sensuous close-ups of tulips in reds, pinks, and yellows.

The house was full of sunlight and warm, bright colors. I

liked the yellow plaid couch in the living room, the dozens of wooden shore birds peeking down from a shelf above the windows in the bedroom, the photograph hanging in his office of Dennis as a young photographer in Gibraltar with a monkey perched on top of his head. I liked his dog, Ty, a big black Lab who followed us from room to room, licking my hand occasionally and wiggling his whole body, including his tail, whenever I looked at him. I had never in my life been so charmed by a man's house. Incredibly, I had also never had a date with a man who owned a dog.

Later we sat outside next to a rushing stream below us at the Bear Café. As the sun set, the mosquitoes came out but we ignored them, absentmindedly slapping at our bare legs as we talked. Dennis told me what he liked about my book.

"I'm attracted to authenticity, openness, honesty in any form," he said.

I was pleased to be perceived as authentic, open, and honest. I never used to think of myself as any of those things. Until I stopped drinking, I lied a lot, mostly about my drinking, but it leached into other areas of my life because to lie about one thing inevitably leads to lying about many things. Instead of saying I was hungover in the morning, I'd say I had the flu. Instead of saying I was going to the liquor store, I'd say I was going to the grocery store. Instead of saying I don't want to go to the movies because they don't sell wine with the popcorn, I'd say I'm too tired to go out. On and on, one lie on top of another. When I stopped drinking, I noticed immediately that there was no longer any need to lie. It was incredibly liberating.

There was something I needed to tell him, something that had bothered me for twenty-four years. After he sold me his

house, he'd asked if he could store some things in the basement for a year because he was going straight to France and
hadn't had time to pack them up to ship. I agreed and then I
discovered his packed boxes filled almost the entire basement. Still, it was only for a year and storing his boxes
seemed like the right thing to do under the circumstances.

During a particularly cold winter a year or two after I'd
bought the house, the boxes were still in the basement and
there was no sign of Dennis Stock returning to fetch them.
The pipes in the house froze and burst, flooding the basement and everything in it. I cleaned up as best I could, leaving the boxes alone to dry out on their own, dismayed about
the damage that might have been done to whatever was in
them. It turned out that leaving them alone had been the
worst thing I could have done because a year or so later, they
bloomed blotches of mildew and fungus.

A friend helped me drag the boxes down from the shelves
and out into the driveway where we opened them one by
one to find nothing but ruined papers, books, and photographs stuck together by huge wads of thick black fungus.
Almost nothing was salvageable so we took most of the
boxes to the dump. One box of books had survived and I
unpacked it and happily incorporated the books into my own
bookshelves. They included a first edition of photographs by
Henri Cartier-Bresson and another book of photographs by
Jacques-Henri Lartigue.

But even better than the books, packed into one of the
boxes I found a twenty-five-pound piece of petrified wood.
I placed it on the floor in the living room and it became one
of my most prized possessions. I say *my* because by then four
years had passed with no communication from Dennis, even

after I'd attempted to contact him twice through his lawyer, who also happened to be my lawyer. Both times the lawyer's letter had been returned stamped ADDRESS UNKNOWN.

I told this to Dennis at dinner, leaving out the part about the one box of good books and the piece of petrified wood that I had kept. So much for my being open and honest.

"I'm sorry," he said, "I must have forgotten I'd left things behind. After selling you the house, I spent the next seven years in Provence, photographing for a book."

He didn't seem that sorry nor did he seem to remember that he had once owned the biggest piece of petrified wood outside of a museum.

"I found you arrogant and intimidating at the closing," I told him. "We had to rush through everything so you could catch your plane to Paris."

"I have no recollection of the closing whatsoever," he said unapologetically.

In 1982 I'd evidently made no impression on this man. In 2006 he was cradling my face in his hand, eager to know me. Timing seems to be everything with men and book publishing. At any rate, I no longer found him arrogant. At dinner I would have described him as simply confident.

"When can I see you again?" he asked.

"Starting the day after tomorrow, I have readings almost every day until the end of June," I told him, "and then a bunch more in July."

"Any nearby?" he asked.

I did have two nearby but did I want Dennis there?

"I read the same passage over and over," I said. "You'll get bored."

"Not at all," he said.

"I'm a nervous wreck when I read," I explained. His presence would make it worse.

"You seemed very relaxed when I saw you," he said.

I'm often told that. It amazes me how well I seem to conceal anxiety.

I admitted I had a reading at Barnes & Noble in Kingston the next week on the evening of June 6.

"But I won't be able to spend time with you," I said. I would be tired because I had a reading outside Boston on the same morning so I'd have to drive for almost four hours to get back to Kingston by six o'clock. Also, a lot of friends had promised to come to the reading that night, including Allie, whom I planned to introduce. If I was not too tired, I'd go out with her afterward to celebrate. It was the wrong night for a second date with Dennis.

"I'll be there," he said, undaunted.

A few minutes later we arrived back at his house and he invited me in for coffee. I declined, relieved that the date was finally over. Why I wanted to escape was not clear to me but I sensed that my life was changing and I had no control over it.

"I don't believe in accidents," Dennis said, standing in his driveway and leaning into my car just before I left.

Hearing him say this just made me want to get away quicker. Maybe because I believed the same thing, and it meant I would have to give up the serenity I had finally found in exchange for the turmoil a relationship was sure to bring. I didn't know if I could bear to do that. I liked having everything my way. I could still remember too vividly what it was like to have no say in my own life. Making my own choices had been a hard-won right.

I drove home and walked into twirling pugs, a smiling Lab, and a talking Siamese cat peeking out at me from between the balustrades halfway up the spiral stairs. Outside the night air was warm and the sound of peepers and bullfrogs floated through the open sliding-glass doors and into the living room. It was not even nine o'clock but I was exhausted and went right upstairs to brush my teeth and get in bed. Lucy heaved a big sigh and settled herself across the foot of the bed. The pugs burrowed under the covers and pinned themselves against me on either side, and the cat curled up between my chin and shoulder, taking up half of my pillow. I could barely move to reach the television remote but found it with my fingertips and clicked the *On* button. I turned the sound way down so it was just loud enough to block any disturbing thoughts about the possibility of overwhelming changes in my life, and fell asleep in the slightly creepy glow of this rumbling tranquilizer. Nobody said turn it up or told me to turn it off or complained about being unable to move with all these animals. Why would I want it any other way?

My brother, Lloyd, my mother, and me, taken just a few months before my mother died.

Grandmother Richards' house in Aiken, South Carolina, where I went to live after my mother died.

Alex, Stephanie, me, and Dorothy in Woodstock.

Lay Me Down,
Georgia, Hotshot,
and Tempo sunning
on a winter morning.

My diva, Georgia.

Luna, Lucy, and Noche on the deck of the house in Olivebridge.

Allie and me with Rinza.

Reading at the Golden
Notebook.

Dennis Stock.

{ 10 }

On Friday, June 2, I was back on the road, heading for Massachusetts to read at Dragon Books in Weston the next day. I would stay with my aunt at her assisted-living apartment where she now lived alone. My uncle has Alzheimer's, which has progressed to the point that he has had to be moved to a facility that offers more care. My aunt bears the loss of her husband of more than fifty years stoically. Never one to dwell on whatever is unpleasant or painful, she spoke of the wonderful people who came to address the residents on an array of subjects from global warming to the state of public education. For years and years she cooked three meals a day for her husband and three children and now seems to enjoy most the luxury of never setting foot in her new kitchen, choosing instead to eat her meals in the dining room of the complex.

I arrived at my aunt's apartment just before dinner and together we took the elevator down one floor and entered an already crowded dining room. I was momentarily depressed at the sight of walkers, wheelchairs, crutches, and canes evident everywhere in the well-appointed, cheerful room. My aunt stopped to introduce me to people as we made our way toward an empty table. I wondered if she was proud that at eighty-seven she can walk unassisted and still drives.

After dinner we sat and talked to two women in their nineties.

"It feels like a prison here," said the one who used to be a lawyer.

"I refuse to sell my house," the other said defiantly. "Someday I'm going home."

I was not really surprised that they felt this way, and it made me sad. Yet it's a beautiful facility and they're lucky they can afford it. It's scary to think about the living conditions that most of the aging population will face, including me. Where will I go in my nineties? No place as elegant as this, I fear.

The next morning I looked out the guest-room window of my aunt's apartment at flocks of Canada geese sitting on the Charles River in the pouring rain. For once I was not mired in feelings about the past. Partly because publishing a book had given me some newfound confidence and partly because I was distracted by worries about the present. It was *pouring,* the kind of rain into which even the hardy would hesitate to venture.

By the time I arrived at Dragon Books at noon, it was raining even harder. Sheets of water were falling from the sky in some kind of apocalyptic nightmare. My aunt, who had arranged this reading, sat in a comfortable chair near the door, ready to greet the forty or so people she had called on my behalf. My cousin Laura was also here, our second meeting in less than a month. Both she and my aunt had known Patience, the owner of the bookstore, for years. They would be greeting people they saw all the time. I would be seeing people I hadn't seen, in some cases, since I was nine. Since the beginning of the book tour, attendance at most of the readings had been low. On this day I was sure *no one* would come out in the bad weather. On top of that, Patience had told me it was to be a book signing, not a reading. On the postcard she had sent out to her customers, it said, *Meet writer Susan Richards.* If I was there to meet people, did that mean I would have to *chat* with them?

I stood in front of a round table stacked with fifty or so of my books and watched the rain blast against the windows as though the whole building were going through a car wash. There were no pedestrians in sight; there were hardly any cars. All that was missing was the tick of a big grandfather clock, echoing into the silence.

A pretty blonde woman and a young girl appeared on the horizon and ran into the store. They were dressed in designer rain gear. The woman was carrying a Prada bag and wearing rubber pink-flowered RHS digger boots, popular with the horsey set. They had not come to *Meet the writer* or even to buy a book. They had come to get dry. They shook the water from their clothes and, after standing near the front door for a while waiting for the rain to end, they gave up and headed for the children's section.

Laura and I leaned against a bookshelf, talking about her still-new relationship. We shared similar anxieties about dating and men. I told her about my dinner date with Dennis, mentioning to her for the first time the peculiarly predestined aspect of the situation. She looked alarmed. I was embarrassed, but the truth was I felt that the relationship already existed.

While we were talking, people my aunt had invited began to arrive, running in out of the rain and piling up their umbrellas by the front door. They paid homage to my aunt in her chair by the door before coming to greet me as I still stood with Laura by the book-laden table. The blonde woman and the young girl stayed on, and suddenly, the store was filled with twenty or so people, laughing about the rain while catching up with me and each other about what they'd been doing for the past five, ten, or thirty years. It was a reunion for many of them as well as for me.

In spite of the terrible weather, more people came to the nonreading at Dragon Books than had come to most of my readings so far. By the time the event was over, Patience said she had sold about forty books. It was only because of my aunt's and Laura's efforts that anyone had come.

I remembered years ago, when we were in our late twenties, walking down Commonwealth Avenue in Boston with Laura, talking about our passion for books. Even in those days we were going to author readings together. I remembered telling her how much I wanted to be a writer and I remembered her answer. "When you get published," she had said, "we'll get everybody to come to your reading."

I recalled so clearly the feeling I had when she said that, the terrible sadness that came over me with the certainty that I would never write a book, never get published. I felt like such a phony telling her I wanted to write while at the same time being sure I never would. And now, all these years later, we had both delivered. Setting aside the issue of talent, the miracle to me, the mystery, is how I quieted all those negative voices in my head long enough to start writing. Part of the answer lies with the deaths of my father and my grandmother, two sources of a relentless and extensive barrage of criticisms directed at my brother and me.

I was thirty and still drinking when my grandmother died, so I was less aware of the mixed feelings I had. At the time I thought I hated her, so her death seemed like the end of a bad story, as though somehow justice had been served. The big bad witch was dead. My brother and I were free of her. Today I can barely recall any of those feelings of animosity toward her. I wish she were still alive so I could thank her for all she did for me, something I never expressed during her life and feel ashamed about now. It sounds like a cliché, but today I realize she did the best she could. Among other things, because of her, I grew up with horses, which means that she gave me the most constant, enduring source of pleasure in my life.

Even so, with her death, I was aware of a certain liberation, the sense that someone who had been watching me with a perpetually wagging finger was finally gone. That feeling was even stronger when my father died, another chronically critical voice who belittled almost everything my brother and I did. Today, it fills me with sadness, not anger, when I remember some of the hurtful things my father did and said. But when he was alive, they were devastating.

He belittled my brother for becoming a lawyer in a small town, for getting married, for saddling himself with children—to my father, all indicators of my brother's failures. I was bad for becoming a teacher because teachers didn't make real money, then for becoming the editor of a small newspaper (no money or prestige), and then for becoming a social worker (same reasons plus who gives a damn about *those people?*). The sons and daughters of his friends were media moguls or the CEOs of big corporations or best-selling authors. He compared us endlessly to his friends' progeny who were making millions, who were players on the world stage. We were an embarrassment.

Since his mother had been our legal guardian and we

hadn't often seen our father, Lloyd and I didn't begin to know him until we were in our twenties. By then our father lived on Pratt Island in Connecticut. After years of destitution because of alcoholism, he had sobered up and made a stunning comeback professionally and financially. But even when his drinking stopped, he'd continued to suffer from depression and from what today I believe would be considered bipolar disorder. Only mental illness could explain why a father would want to undermine his children so completely. He had tremendous mood swings and when we went to visit him, we never knew who would greet us at the door—the morose, no-energy father or the hyped-up, full of world-changing ideas father. But each expressed regret that he'd ever had children and disappointment in those children.

Perversely, my brother and I both loved this man. But with his death when I was forty-one years old, I distinctly remembered that, along with sadness, I felt freed. There was no one left in the world who could make me feel as deeply ashamed of myself as my father and grandmother had. I could make a decision and not look over my shoulder awaiting the derision that would follow. I could breathe. It was no coincidence that shortly after my father's death, I took my first writing workshop.

I can't help wondering sometimes what my father would think of my book if he were alive. He had always wanted to be a writer and had once, in his new sobriety, taken a class in screenwriting at the New School in New York City. I think he had tremendous talent, but he lacked the discipline required to sit down, write, and then endlessly revise. As for what he would think of my book? It takes no effort at all for me to hear his scathing criticism in my head.

*   *   *

LATER THAT AFTERNOON, I said goodbye to my aunt and
Laura and headed for the Cohasset Harbor Inn, on the southern shore of Massachusetts, a little more than an hour's drive
away. I had a 9:45 breakfast reading at the Atlantica Restaurant
hosted by Buttonwood Books the next day. I'd be joining
seasoned authors James Dodson and Elinor Lipman for this
annual event.

Near dusk, I left the highway and started following detour
signs around major road construction toward what I hoped
would eventually be the town of Cohasset. I drove and drove,
watching the houses get bigger and bigger, until it felt as if I
had left the real world and arrived on the planet Rich-R-Us.
I went slowly, taking in the mansions on the water, every one
of them gorgeous. I was lost in the land of giant houses, following the road as it wound in and out of small coves along
the coastline, pulling over to let the occasional car pass so
I could gawk. Just before dark, I found the Cohasset Inn.
Once again, Kathy had booked a beautiful room that overlooked Cohasset Harbor, which was filled with sailboats
tied at their moorings on a glassy sea. It was the third time
I'd stayed at a hotel since the book tour began and I felt the
same thing I always felt when I was alone in a hotel—utterly
disconnected from my own life. Loneliness is only part of it.
I felt like a balloon that someone had let go of, suspended
in endless nothingness. The experience made me feel mildly
agoraphobic, as though without familiar reference points I
didn't exist. Thank God for the Internet. The best antidote
to this feeling was to read and send e-mails. I dragged out
my computer and began connecting, literally and metaphorically. I spent the rest of the night at the computer, not even

venturing out for food. I suppose I was feeding myself in a more important way.

The next morning I drove to the restaurant filled with the usual prereading anxiety. The first indication that this one would be different was the number of cars backed up along the road waiting to get into the restaurant parking lot. It looked like a wedding or a funeral procession but they were here, obviously, to see Elinor and James. Only well-established authors could command a turnout like this. I was both pleased and troubled to be riding in on their coattails. It would be good for my book to get this kind of exposure, but I couldn't help wondering how the two of them would feel about sharing the podium with a newcomer.

I was greeted by the event's coordinator, Totsie. After shaking my hand, she continued to hold it in hers while she told me how much she'd enjoyed my book.

"You'll be sitting right there," she said, pointing to a round table in the middle of the large dining room where seven women were already seated and talking. There were at least ten such tables and maybe as many as a hundred women, who all seemed to know each other. Now I was to be thrown into their midst. I had imagined the three authors would sit together on a dais, separate from the audience and from each other so as to make talking difficult. We would shake hands and smile at each other but real conversation would be impossible. No one would discover the impostor in the room.

I made my way to the table and sat down. I could not believe this was happening to me, that I would have to *talk* with people I didn't know. But to my great relief, after we were introduced, the women at the table continued speaking with each other. Just when I thought, *OK, I can handle this*, the gracious owner of Buttonwood Books, Betsey Detwiler, came over to explain the morning's format. We were each to speak for twenty minutes and then take questions.

"Talk?"

"You know," she said cheerily, "about how you came to write this book. But don't just read."

No one had told me this wasn't a reading; could Kathy have forgotten? Had I? I had prepared nothing and could not speak extemporaneously about anything except possibly acute anxiety.

I nodded dumbly, knowing I had no choice but to read. I'd be lucky if I could manage that.

When Elinor Lipman entered the dining room, I recognized her immediately from her book-jacket photos. She was small and thin and exuded confidence and intelligence as she strode across the room, stopping at several tables along the way to chat with appreciative readers. She spotted James Dodson and joined him. Led by Betsey, Elinor and James came over to my table, and we were introduced. I told Elinor how much I loved her books, how exciting it was to meet her. She was friendly and warm. We were both wearing big red necklaces.

"I haven't read your book," James said, "but I've heard wonderful things about it." He was the embodiment of southern charm.

"Who wants to speak first?" Betsey asked.

The question triggered a hot flash and I could feel the sweat gathering at my temples and everywhere clothing touched my skin. In a minute, I was completely damp. I don't know who spoke first, I only know that I was last.

Suddenly, it was my turn at the podium in front of the biggest crowd I had ever faced. My voice shook as I explained that I had written a book to tell how caring for a sick horse had led me to understand that repressed grief had stifled my life. My "speech" lasted only a few minutes and then I read for the rest of my allotted time. I was so overcome at breaking the rules that I started to cry as I read. The only thing worse than reading in front of a hundred strangers is crying in front of them. I read on through the tears, utterly humiliated.

When I finished reading, there were a few questions. As I answered them, my tears stopped. But if I could have made a run for the door, I would have. I was thankful when Betsey brought the questions to an end, and herded Elinor, James, and me to a table in the back of the restaurant, where we sat behind stacks of our books so people could purchase them and have them signed.

I sat between James and Elinor, envisioning long lines forming in front of the table on either side with no line at all in front me. Miraculously, that didn't happen; the three lines seemed to be about equal. Time after time as people approached the table, they said things to me like, "Are you OK?" and "It really looked rough for you up there." The voices were kind but I was still ashamed.

Each of us sold most of the books stacked in front of us. It was a good feeling for many reasons but mostly because it meant I could leave. Betsey had given each of us a Buttonwood Books canvas tote bag, which contained newspaper clippings with reviews of our books, announcements about this event, and, best of all, copies of each other's books. After Elinor and James signed their books for me, I stood with my new tote bag over my shoulder, ready to say thank you and goodbye.

"What?" said Betsey, looking upset. "Aren't you going to stay for the lunch."

I didn't think I could possibly manage to spend another hour or more there, especially at a formal luncheon where I would have to eat and make small talk like a normal human being.

"I have a 6:00 p.m. reading tonight in Kingston, New York," I said as an excuse.

Unfortunately, Betsey knew her geography. "If you leave by two, you'll still be there an hour early," she said. "Besides," she added, lowering her voice, "they've prepared such a nice lunch, especially for us."

What could I say? A few minutes later I was seated at a table set with white linen and nice china, looking at the harbor while Betsey gave a toast to the authors (I toasted with a seltzer). The social ordeal wasn't as bad as I'd imagined and by three, I was back in my car, following that of a bookstore employee who had kindly volunteered to lead me through the confusion of detours and road construction back to the main highway.

In retrospect, it had been a wonderful event. A few weeks later, I received a personal letter from Totsie, thanking me. Included was a photograph of me standing at the podium, appearing to smile as I spoke to the audience. It is a record of how calm I look in the middle of a full-blown anxiety attack.

ON THE DRIVE to Kingston, I wondered if menopause was the reason I'd cried during the reading. Anxiety isn't new, but the crying is. I seem to cry a lot, maybe as often as once a day at things that ordinarily wouldn't move me to tears: sentimental music played during an ad on television, a happy ending to a story, a pretty sunset. Tears are like hot flashes; they come without warning, regardless of whether I'm with people or not. The worst hot flashes are the ones I get while I'm teaching. There I am, trapped in front of twenty students, turning bright red while little beads of sweat gather along my forehead and temples. I'm forever throwing open the windows while my students huddle in parkas and hats, horrified at the cold rush of air suddenly pouring over them.

"This is what fifty-six feels like," I explain, standing in the frigid air, fanning myself with a notebook.

"You're just like my mother," one of them said once, "she's crazy, too."

I've always felt crazy but menopause adds a new element. Tears are not all bad either. Crying is at least purgative. Afterward I feel better. Something bottled up has been expelled even if I don't understand what it is.

I wondered if I'd cry that night in Kingston. This would be a landmark reading for me, my first big bookstore, a Barnes & Noble, and the biggest venue on my home turf. Many friends had said they would be there. I wanted to perform especially well.

The closer I got to Kingston, the more anxious I became. It was a longer drive than I'd expected and I arrived literally minutes before the reading was scheduled to begin. I was comforted by the fact that I'd been to several readings at Barnes & Noble stores in the past few months and none of them had started on time. I also reminded myself that since I was the reader, it couldn't begin without me.

I pulled into the parking lot at five minutes to seven. As I walked to the door, I saw a big photograph of me and a display of my books in the front window. It had been there for about two weeks but I still had to catch my breath every time I saw it. Quite simply, it amazed me. It didn't seem possible that a book I'd written was stacked by the dozen in a Barnes & Noble window. I'd also just learned that it was a *Discover Great New Writers* pick and a July Book Sense pick; it had been honored both by Barnes & Noble and by our country's independent booksellers. I'd never heard of either award before my book was chosen. It all seemed like a wonderful accident.

I pushed open the big front doors and saw the place where I would be reading, one of the relatively open areas of the store in front of a wall of cookbooks. Already there were twenty or more people sitting in the semicircle of chairs and I glimpsed many I knew wandering around the store. I spotted Rich, the store manager, carrying a mic and an amplifier over to the reading area. So far, the only disconcerting element was that the first few rows were filled by my current and former students. I was deeply embarrassed to be reading a section that deals with the experience of trying on bras at Victoria's Secret. The last thing a teacher wants to talk about with her students is the state of her underwear. I briefly considered reading another section—something less personal. But I was too anxious to think clearly and also afraid that reading something else would make me cry.

Rich fiddled with the mic, trying to get it to stop squeaking. Friends came to greet me, and several people, including some students, brought me flowers. No one had ever given me flowers at a reading before. I saw Elaine arrive, escorting our friend Delores, who is in her nineties. Then I noticed Dennis and immediately my anxiety level doubled. I could barely look at him except to nod hello.

We ran out of chairs, even after Rich brought extras from

the back. People leaned against the book stacks, filling the aisles all around that section of the store. There were many familiar faces but also many unfamiliar ones. At twenty past seven, Rich came back to tell me that this was the largest crowd ever gathered for a reading at the Barnes & Noble in Kingston. He estimated that there were about seventy people so far and more were arriving. He suggested we begin and then gave me the briefest introduction I'd ever received: "And now Susan Richards will read from her memoir."

A wave of exhaustion swept over me and I wondered if I could do this. I thought about sitting to read. Instead, I picked up the mic and when I turned it on, it didn't squeak, and I could speak softly and still be heard. I was acutely aware of two people in the audience: Dennis and Nan, the freelance editor I've worked with over the years. One was a comfort and one wasn't. To get through the reading, I focused on Nan and tried to block out Dennis. I wished he weren't there. His mere presence felt like a claim on me. Yet even as I thought this, I knew it was absurd. But I could feel the tears building up and that made me forget about Dennis and everything else. I was determined not to cry again; I put all my effort into *forbidding* myself to cry.

When the reading was over it felt as if the whole book tour was over. I was so relieved not to be reading again anywhere near where I live that it was as if some dreadful curse had been lifted. I was almost giddy with joy. I didn't know how oppressed I'd felt until it was over. In spite of how supportive my friends and colleagues had been, here, near my own home, was where my fear that *no one would come* was the strongest. I had been living with that dread for months, ever since the three local readings had been booked in March. Then, like that night, when the miracle happened and people came, I was overwhelmed with a mix of love, gratitude, and shame. The shame was so deep, so strong. I am sure it was at least partly responsible for my tears. To be honored that way, to be the center for a moment of what felt like a big loving family, was for me, to be too close to the fire, too close to a heat I find hard to bear. The sense of *belonging* was so overpowering that I had to postpone savoring it until I was home, in bed surrounded by my dogs, listening to the sounds of the night.

People lined up to buy books and have them signed and I talked with everyone, whether I knew them or not. With relief flooding through me, I'd never been so chatty. At one point I looked up, wondering where Allie was, and then I remembered: I hadn't introduced her. I had told her I was going to and then I had forgotten. I felt terrible. Immediately, I realized that she had left because she was hurt. How could I possibly have forgotten to introduce her? She'd even worn a new necklace she'd made from beads we'd bought together from our favorite bead store. The necklace featured a small carved wooden horse, perfect for an evening with a horse theme.

I finished signing books with a heart made heavy by my thoughtlessness. So often I'd hear from people after they'd read *Chosen by a Horse* about how kind they thought I must be, how good. When I thought of what I had done to Allie, it made me cringe.

Dennis stayed in his chair until the last person in line left and I was alone at the table with the flowers and cards. He was wearing the same yellow raincoat he had worn when I first saw him at the Catskill Animal Sanctuary. He was impossible to miss in a crowd.

He approached and presented me with flowers. "You're a natural speaker," he told me and hugged me hard.

"It's all an act," I said, too tired to care what he thought of that. But it was true. There's nothing natural for me about reading in front of a lot of people.

"I'd love to take you for dinner somewhere," he said. "You must be hungry."

I was so tired that the idea of eating struck me as preposterous. I shook my head. "I'm sorry," I said, "I'm too tired to go out."

"What about talking for a minute?" he said, nodding toward the tables at the Starbucks café.

I agreed to stay for a minute and he helped me gather up and carry the flowers and cards to a small table. He ordered a coffee and I got bottled water. Just as we sat down, one of my students came over to the table and presented me with more flowers.

Dennis asked me when we could get together again. We pulled out our calendars. Between my readings and his trip to Europe, we had only one available day in the whole month of June, the next Sunday. But Dennis leaned across the table to look at my schedule and saw that I had another reading across the river in Rhinebeck the next Saturday. He offered to drive me to this reading and suggested we have dinner afterward. If I agreed, it would be his third time at one of my readings.

"You'll be so bored," I said.

"Not at all," he answered. "I won't even be there." He said he would wander around town while I read.

This seemed OK and we agreed to meet halfway to Rhinebeck, where we'd leave my car and go the rest of the way in his. We talked for another fifteen minutes and then it was time for me to go home. As we walked to my car, he tried one more time to persuade me to join him for a quick dinner. But that night it was so out of the question, I didn't even respond.

"See you Saturday," I said as I slid into my car.

Before I left, he leaned into my open window and said, "Are you really going to make me eat Chinese food by myself?"

His persistence was funny, and we both laughed.

"I really am," I said.

On the way home I was aware again of the feeling that the relationship with Dennis Stock had already "happened" and that we were filling in the pages of an already written story. He must have felt something similar because the next morning I woke up to this e-mail from him.

I sat there last night with a growing admiration and affection. The persona of writer/teacher was so very apparent. My feelings of pride and attraction for you grew by leaps and bounds. Your telling the audience why you wrote the book, punctuated by nods to arriving friends made my heart melt. Your delicate balance of the need to be grounded during a professional responsibility was so apparent. A groupie I ain't, but when I witnessed this smooth control after your tiring day, I was caught, as they say, hook, line and sinker. Call today if you get a chance. See you soon.

D

I am embarrassed to say that I answered this lovely e-mail rather flippantly. I wrote, *Thank you for your kind words but I never use the phone unless I have to—Susan*

Dennis's boldness scared me and at the same time I liked it. It made me want to sell the house and run away. Or call him up and say, *Let's just move in together and get it over with.* Instead, I shoved aside these contradictory feelings and called Allie to apologize. We'd never really had a fight so this was our first strained phone call in twenty years.

Many of the e-mails and letters readers sent me spoke of Allie and how wonderful she seemed, how lucky I was to have such a friendship. I'd read a few of them to her but there were many more that I hadn't. My plan was to Xerox them someday and give them to her. I hadn't even kept up with telling her about them. Both she and Elaine had pointed out that I didn't call anymore. I'd never been good about calling, but it had gotten worse, they said. I think they were both sick of hearing how overwhelmed I felt.

Allie and I talked for a few minutes but didn't resolve anything. Instead, it was one of those moments in a relationship when something permanently shifts. I didn't know if the alteration could be undone. I wondered again if, now that the book was out, she'd had second thoughts about being so exposed, about being written about.

Weeks before, Allie, Elaine, another friend, Barbara, and I had made tentative plans to go to the Mount, Edith Wharton's home in western Massachusetts, which is now a museum. The date we'd chosen was June 13, right in the middle of the book tour, but I'd agreed because I wanted to spend a day with three good friends and because I loved visiting the shrine of any beloved author. Before we hung up, Allie and I agreed to keep this date. I hoped that spending the day together would help ameliorate whatever had happened. And, thankfully, it did.

I spent the next day trying to catch up with e-mails, paying bills, and, more important to me than anything, taking the dogs for a good long walk. I had a reading later that night at another Barnes & Noble an hour away in the town of Newburgh. But the day was mine and since it was hot, I took the dogs on one of their favorite walks through the woods following a path along a stream. Lucy and Luna jumped in and out of the water along the way while Noche stood on the bank making his bird screams whenever they left him behind. It was pure joy to watch them run through the woods together, splashing in and out of the water. At one point I picked Noche up and, still wearing my sneakers, waded into the stream to hold him suspended in the water to cool him off. While I was holding him, he wagged his tail and licked me, such a sweet sign of trust. He knew I wouldn't let him go.

The reading in Newburgh later was a disaster. Again, it absolutely poured. A handful of friends showed up, including Elaine and Francis, and my agent also came. In addition to this small group of acquaintances, there were two women I'd never met. Fewer than ten people in a very big store. When the reading was over we stood around and talked and one of the women said, "It's such a good book. I don't understand why attendance was so bad."

"Bad?" scoffed Helen, the über-agent. "There were nine of us on a lousy, rainy night. I'd call that a big success."

A big success? How could I not love her?

I reached home tired and a little depressed but before I went to bed, I checked my e-mails and found this waiting for me from Dennis.

* * *

Susan dear, I have a friend who believes that there are no accidents. Therefore, our fate is predetermined. I never gave it much thought until I met you and as we both know something special is going on. Perhaps it is simply that two decent people, in the period of their lives when luck in loving another is an unusual circumstance, have been offered a gift for reasons we will never know. This gift does not come without responsibilities I think.

I suggest that compromise and negotiation are part and parcel of the requirement for our special circumstances to grow. I feel that you are exciting and worth any reasonable effort on my part to pursue success in making us a true couple. When you say you are reluctant to talk on the phone it causes consternation. I enjoy hearing your voice because it reveals charm and how you feel which gives me a chance to support your needs when necessary. Conversations by phone with true friends is our way of saying "I'm there for you." I want to be there for you no matter where we end up because I think you need it and deserve it. Please try to use the phone as an instrument to share the day with someone who cares.

I have reserved a table for us on Saturday at 8:30 at the Terrapin.

D

I felt trapped by this e-mail, forced to accept its logic, its gentle prodding. He so clearly had articulated the challenge for me, the challenge of any relationship: compromise and negotiation, two elements that were lacking in my dealings with previous partners. I was so bad at both and the men I had known had been even worse. The absence of these skills had always spelled doom.

But there was something thrilling about a man who threw these two words into an e-mail so early in the game or, for that matter, who used them at all. Should I hold fast to the notion that compromise and negotiation were not part of my genetic makeup? That is, did I continue to be the one in a relationship who gave in, so my own identity was sacrificed? Would negotiating always mean the few minutes it took before I succumbed?

As trapped as I felt by this e-mail, forced to make decisions, I also felt invited into a new world, offered a new set of possibilities as appealing as they were unfamiliar. A man who *might* consider my thoughts, my feelings, my priorities? At the very least it would require that I express them first. And then what? To be honest, I couldn't even imagine it, the same way I couldn't imagine what it felt like to have a mother, or a father who ever said one kind thing. It made me dizzy when I tried. Literally. Unless you've never been shown consideration, you can't know the impact of such treatment. But here they were being offered to me, compromise and negotiation, a chance to be seen by another, a chance to be *considered*.

I decided to take those words for what they surely must be, for what Dennis had so rightly called a gift. It was a gift as precious and rare as any I'd ever received.

{ 11 }

On Thursday night at seven o'clock I walked into the Barnes & Noble in Poughkeepsie, the same store where Michael Korda had once read for only ten people. As it turned out, Michael was the lucky one.

I read before seven.

Saturday night in Rhinebeck felt like a festival. The city people were up for the weekend, restaurants were packed, and a line of people snaked down the block, waiting to get into Upstate Films. It was warm and sunny and Dennis found a convenient parking space right in a town in which parking is impossible.

"You have parking karma," I said, impressed. We'd left my car in Kingston and come the rest of the way in his. He was the first man I'd dated who didn't drive too fast. Paul had driven so fast that on our second date I'd told him that the only way I could continue to see him was if I drove. Amazingly, he'd agreed, and for six years, I did all the driving.

"Shall we look around?" Dennis asked.

We were half an hour early for my reading so Dennis took my arm in his, and we began to wander in and out of stores. This was something else I'd never, ever done with a date. The only man I knew who enjoyed purposeless shopping was my brother, Lloyd. My brother is as much fun to shop with as any of my women friends.

I paused at a jewelry counter to look at a necklace of big yellow glass beads strung on a piece of rawhide.

"They'd look lovely hanging in a window with light coming through them," Dennis said.

That was something my grandmother would have done, hung a necklace in a window to catch the light. She displayed her jewelry all over the house, on walls in every single room including the bathrooms. If it wasn't on her neck or wrist, it was on a wall somewhere, in plain sight. A lot of it was like this glass bead necklace but she'd hung the diamonds and sapphires, too. She was democratic when it came to jewelry; every piece was equal in her eyes.

We stopped at the window of a real estate office covered with photographs of houses for sale and pointed at the ones we liked or didn't like. We agreed that there was nothing more beautiful than a barn or a house that looked like a barn. Next to jewelry, houses were my favorite thing to window shop for. Whenever I'm in a new city for the first time, I collect all the free real estate booklets and stop at the window of every broker's office I pass to look. It's probably a good thing I'm not rich or I'd have dozens of houses all over the world. And too much jewelry.

We almost escaped a bakery but were pulled back by the smell of something irresistible. We went in and I chose a molasses cookie and Dennis, a scone. We ate these while we slowly made our way toward the bookstore. Selfishly, I liked that he had a sweet tooth because I do, too, and it was something I felt guilty about. If I was really interested in healthy eating (as I always claimed to be), I wouldn't eat sweets as often as I do.

We arrived at the bookstore five minutes before the reading was scheduled to begin. Dennis disappeared into the stacks while I stopped at the counter to introduce myself. I was given a warm welcome by two staff members who said they expected a good crowd. I didn't know what a good crowd there meant. A month before, chef and author Mario Batali had been there and the line to see him stretched all the way down the block. It was a small store and they had cleared an area in the middle where they had set up a wooden podium and about fifteen folding chairs. As I waited to begin, most of the chairs filled up and a few people leaned against the wall in the back. It wasn't a line snaking around the block but it was a good crowd and I was grateful. Dennis waved as he left to wander around town. Just then, my horse vet, Amy Grice, arrived. She had brought a friend and they sat in the front row. This time I didn't make the same mistake I'd made with Allie; I introduced Amy and explained the importance of her role in the memoir.

The reading and signing went smoothly and, when it was over, a few people lingered to talk. A woman who'd openly cried during the reading stayed to tell me how much the book meant to her. She, too, owned a horse she adored, and she opened her purse and pulled out a photograph of him. Another woman spoke of her efforts to date men after being single for a long time; another about how hard it was to take care of her dying father. These are the things people speak about most often at my readings: horses, dating, and death. Alcoholism and abuse are sometimes topics, too. It always surprises me how intense these informal talk sessions can become, how personal.

Later, over dinner, I remarked about this to Dennis.

"People read the book and feel they know you," he said.

I never imagined that because I was open in a book, readers might be equally open with me. My fear was that some would mistakenly believe I had answers, that I had written the book because I was "healed" from something. I don't feel healed. What I do feel is that I have a better understanding of myself and that Lay Me Down was the catalyst for that, the teacher. She showed me a part of myself I hadn't known existed: a woman full of forty-year-old grief and anger. It seemed as profound to me as suddenly discovering that walking had been difficult all those years because I was missing a leg. The missing leg would not heal, but metaphorically speaking, walking could improve with the aid of crutches or a prosthesis. And with the ability to walk better, I could take new risks that wouldn't have been possible before. In that sense, my life had changed.

I often wonder what else I'm not aware of, what other limitations I have that keep me from moving forward more boldly. I'm sure there are many, and I only hope I am lucky enough to continue to find teachers as gentle as Lay Me Down to show me the way.

Over dinner, Dennis and I conversed easily. I told him how unnerved I was by the readings and that I hadn't expected them to be so difficult. I also told him that in spite of the hefty sale of the paperback rights to Harcourt, trying to live the writing life often felt like a gigantic financial folly. Dennis said he had been taking such risks since dropping out of high school to apprentice for *Life* magazine photographer Gjon Mili.

"Did you ever wonder if you were good enough, whether you'd made a mistake?" I asked him, thinking of all the years I'd doubted myself as a writer.

"Not at all," he said and told me about an incident that had happened while he was still working at *Life*. He was walking back from lunch with his boss, and just as they were crossing Broadway, Mili had turned to Dennis and said, "You'll never make it as a photographer."

Instead of hearing that as "Sorry, try real estate," which is what Mili meant, Dennis's silent retort was, "He's right, I'll never make it as a *Life* photographer." Four years later he was invited to join the most prestigious group of photographers in the world, Magnum Photos, so he left *Life* and went out on his own and has never looked back, in spite of many years of financial hardship.

It was thrilling to talk to someone who had made his art his life, who'd never doubted his calling. What I had taken for arrogance twenty-four years ago I now saw as enormous confidence, not just in his work, but in his own thoughts and opinions. This was someone who *knew* himself and, more astonishing still, liked himself. I came from a long line of self-doubters, so to see such self-assurance in another was as appealing as it was unfamiliar.

Dinner was over and we were sipping good decaf when Dennis said, "The idea of not seeing you for a month is painful."

I was beginning to feel the same way. "I'm going to a horse show tomorrow," I said. "Want to come?"

A world-class hunter/jumper facility had recently been built in the nearby town of Saugerties for the HITS (Horse Shows in the Sun) show circuit and I'd been going to sit in the grass and look at the most beautiful horses in the world every chance I got ever since. There was a time when I wouldn't have noticed the one-dimensionality of the crowd that frequented the events—and it would be a crowd, with fourteen barns housing over eleven hundred horses—but there was no question that I now felt a pang at seeing such a concentration of wealth in a world with so much poverty and suffering.

I was afraid Dennis would think that I delighted in this display of luxury when the truth was, I went in spite of it because *I couldn't resist the horses.* Allie and I sometimes went together and, rather than watch the competition in the main ring, we'd sit in the shade of the dining pavilion, sharing a paper boat of greasy french fries while watching the most magnificent horses in the world warm up in the practice ring fifteen feet away. They cantered in graceful circles before us, a heartbreakingly beautiful parade of different breeds and colors. We gaped. Sometimes we cried. The truth was, if either of us had had it, we'd have spent a hundred thousand dollars on one of those horses in a minute. Perhaps money is all that really stands between me and complete hypocrisy.

Dennis had never heard of HITS but seemed happy at the idea of spending an afternoon together anywhere. He dropped me off at my car after dinner and, for the first time, I felt tension around the issue of how to say good night. Since the onset of menopause, the state of my libido could best be described as nonexistent. Allie claimed that could change, that a libido could be jump-started by the right person. I was skeptical. Most of the menopausal women I knew said they too had experienced this drop in libido. The only ones who still had a sex drive seemed to be the women taking hormone replacements.

So there I was with my dead libido standing in the parking lot saying good night to a man who clearly still had *his*. What to do? On top of that, Dennis was one of those men who *exude* sexuality. Ironically, it was part of his enormous appeal, even though my responders seemed to have gone missing. Both of us knew we were past the peck-on-the-cheek stage but what were the options for such mismatched chemistry? I had no desire to fake enthusiasm, so I decided to take the honest approach and keep our kiss on the lips as chaste as such a thing could be by making it quick. When Dennis looked disappointed, I decided to say something.

"Whatever's happening between us doesn't feel sexual to me right now," I said. "If that's a problem for you, I would understand."

"Not at all," he said, ever the gentleman. "I'm content just to be in your company."

His response felt honest and not honest at the same time. What I sensed to be true was that he was willing to give it some time. Fair enough.

When I arrived home there was an e-mail from him waiting.

Please don't be frightened about your readings. They are truly appealing to the audience. Just see them as a necessary chore in getting recognition for future published books. Most authors of note make public appearances and are no more skilled than you with your lovely simple approach. You hooked me. Hopefully you will discover that having someone who cares about your welfare will soothe a corner of your soul, thereby freeing up the rest of you to write your heart out. Freelancing is a rough ride even when success appears on the horizon. So please take solace in the fact that your level of intelligence will always find a way to survive financially.

xxxxx D

I was relieved that there was no reference to our brief discussion about sex. His e-mail was caring and pressure free. Still, I wondered about the future, about that aspect of our relationship. Was ours to be a platonic love? This didn't seem likely with a man like Dennis.

"Don't worry about it," Allie said on the phone when I called to suggest that she come to HITS so she could meet Dennis. "The issue of sex will resolve itself in time."

This seemed possible, so we dropped the subject and agreed to meet at the food pavilion later that afternoon.

JUST BEFORE I left to meet Dennis at his house, I received an e-mail from my brother.

I checked out Dennis on the Magnum website and his work is impressive. BTW, his date of birth is 1928, making him almost 78, not 68 as you said. Are you aware of this?

I was not aware of it, and it almost took my breath away. When I'd Googled him, I'd seen 1928 and then must have done the math wrong. I scribbled down the numbers on a piece of scrap paper and, of course, discovered that my brother was right. Dennis was seventy-eight, not sixty-eight. In a second everything changed. Seventy-eight was old. Sixty-eight? Not quite. He didn't look seventy-eight, nowhere near it. He exuded energy and strength and he was strikingly handsome. It was hard to believe. What did it mean, dating a seventy-eight-year-old man? What would I face? What would he face? The word that kept coming to mind was death. The issue at seventy-eight, no matter what else was going on, must surely be the imminence of your own mortality. I called Allie back.

"I'm dating a man who could drop dead at lunch with us today," I told her and explained about the age mistake.

"That seems a tad dramatic," she said. "He could outlive you."

"Seventy-eight isn't important?" This was more a challenge than a question. Part of me wanted her to convince me that seventy-eight was meaningless.

"Look," she said, sighing, "do you like this guy?"

"Of course," I said.

"Well, then just *relax*. Anyway, I want to meet him. I'll tell you what I think after, OK?"

A little while later I arrived at Dennis's house to find he had tripped and fallen over one of the unpacked boxes still stacked in his living room.

See. He is going to kill himself in his own house. It's such a seventy-eight-year-old thing to do, I thought to myself.

His ankle was badly discolored and swollen. I wondered if it would be possible for him to walk around the vast grounds of HITS. He assured me he could and even insisted on driving, so off we went, Dennis loaded with several cameras, and me laden with fresh misgivings.

Once there, we made our way from the parking area to the show grounds. It was a long walk on a narrow path and along the way we passed dozens of horses and riders coming and going from the show and practice rings. Dennis moved so slowly that several times I was worried that he'd be crushed by a horse. I envisioned it as a sort of tabloid photo of an old man flattened under the hoof of a nostril-flaring Thoroughbred glaring into the camera with a guiltless, haughty eye. Like their owners, these horses seemed to exude an air of entitlement. I found myself keeping a firm grip on Dennis's elbow, pulling him toward the edge of the path for safety.

"I suspect I'm being helped along," he said.

I was embarrassed that he'd noticed. "Your ankle must hurt," I replied, trying not to sound ageist.

We escaped being crushed and arrived safely at the heart of HITS. For a few moments we stood together in the middle of a dusty intersection, transfixed by the scene. For a moment I forgot that Dennis was seventy-eight years old and basked in the knowledge that he was as bowled over as I was. If horse was your religion, this was the Vatican, a place where the ideal became manifest, a pageant of equine pulchritude. Something happens to me around horses and it happened here, in the middle of HITS on this sunny June day as I gripped Dennis's elbow. Very simply, I was filled with love, a pulsing, heat-filled ache of such tenderness, I was transformed. I am a better person around horses. I am the good Susan, or so it feels. Certainly, I am the happy Susan.

"Extraordinary," Dennis said as we stared.

We were standing in the middle of the busiest intersection in the whole two-hundred-acre facility. A quarter of a mile behind us was a group of some of the nicer barns; on one side of the road almost as far as the eye could see were show rings filled with horses and riders; on the other side of the road stood the food pavilion, the main practice ring, and a series of equine-related shops. Past that were the two main show rings surrounded by hand-built stone walls and filled with what looked like fine white sand but was really crushed rubber. The land had been built up around the two main rings so spectators could either sit in the bleachers or along the grassy banks for a perfect birds-eye view of the ring below. In the far distance, visible from anywhere at HITS, was a glorious view of the Catskill Mountains.

A steady parade of horses and riders strolled past us, the arrogance of all palpable but only forgivable in the horses.

"There's a story here," Dennis said, thinking out loud about a possible photo essay, "but I'm not sure I'm inclined to tell it."

I knew exactly what he meant. He, too, was aware of the mind-boggling display of wealth and privilege surrounding us.

We made our cautious way down the dirt road, stopping often to admire a horse, a pony, a snoring black Lab slumped across the steering wheel of a parked golf cart. We breathed air filled with the smell of grilling hamburgers, manure, and leather carried on the dust kicked up by dozens of golf carts and scooters whirring past us as they transported competitors, coaches, and laborers between the show rings and barns. Mexican immigrants walked riderless horses draped in monogrammed sweat sheets to cool them down after a workout or to warm them up before being ridden.

The horses were unfazed by the mayhem surrounding them. These were the top equine athletes in the world and had, for the most part, been patiently and lovingly trained to accept the commotion of the show world. Their eyes and posture said it all. Most stood quietly at the end of a slack lead line, head and neck stretched long and low, with blinking, sleepy eyes. Their ears were up and forward, attentive to but not anxious about their surroundings. Every one of them was a study in equine perfection.

I pointed and sighed and said *Look* way too much but Dennis accepted it all with good humor. We sat under a canvas tent and watched horses compete in the main ring for a while. Every horse that competed in this ring was a top athlete but the same could not always be said of the riders.

At around two, we headed toward the food pavilion to meet Allie. As we approached, I saw her and she spotted me and beckoned to us. As Dennis and I walked through the maze of tables, Allie watched. I knew she was wondering about his limp. Sure enough, as soon as the introductions were over, Allie leaned forward, pulled up his pants leg, and said, "What did you do to this ankle?"

Her familiarity might have been offensive if her concern hadn't been so genuine. She pulled his ankle into her lap while gently guiding it through a range of motion exercises.

"Ouch," Dennis said and explained about tripping over the boxes.

She stopped rotating his foot and applied pressure near his ankle bone with her thumb. "This will hurt for a minute," she said, "but it will help get things moving in there."

I had no idea what she meant and I don't think Dennis did either. Still, this is what she does for a living; she "gets things moving." A massage therapist works with lots of people who are injured one way or another. After living for more than twenty years with a bad back, I credit Allie with keeping me upright.

She fiddled with his ankle while we talked and watched horses warm up in the ring in front of us. Most of the horses are tall, leggy, and muscular—the equine equivalent of professional basketball players in body type. But it's the shorter, scrappy-looking horses that make us throw our hands across our hearts and sigh. These are the Morgans, the quarter horses, and the who-knows-what-they-ares. They're the underdogs, the ones you look at and think, *How did he get here?* These were the ones we rooted for. The women riders are often better than the men, more graceful, more in sync with their horses. But grace doesn't count in this sport, only how fast you can clear a series of jumps without knocking any down. Still, we appreciated a "good seat" and disdained the riders who bounced around. The ones who earned our deepest scorn cantered by while talking on their cell phones.

I could tell Allie liked Dennis. She was animated and chatty, giving him advice about icing his ankle and herbs he could take to reduce the swelling. When we left Dennis alone at the table to bring a pizza back from the food court, she said, "This is the one. I just have a feeling."

I didn't necessarily trust Allie's feeling. For years she had hoped against hope that I would find the right man. It was a hope that came from a loving, caring place, but I thought her desire might color her ability to judge the caliber of the candidate. "You say that every time I meet someone," I said.

"Never," she said emphatically, "I've *never* said that before."

The truth was, I didn't remember whether she'd ever said, *He's the one* before or not. Menopause was slowly making a mockery of memory.

"What about his age?" I asked. This was what mattered to me now.

"I just don't think age is an issue. He's *so* interesting."

He *was* interesting. He was an interesting seventy-eight-year old. All my life I'd had abandonment issues. I couldn't help it—it was the result of losing too much too soon. A whole family at age five. It had made me cautious, sometimes in the dumbest ways, but always for the same reason: to survive. I knew how to live alone. I'd learned early. What would happen now if I became attached to someone, if I really cared, and then he died? Grief had almost killed me the first time. Ultimately, I protected myself the only way I knew how. I went dead inside. *Dead.* I didn't want to go dead again. I'd had another taste of it when Lay Me Down died and a stronger dose when I'd lost Georgia—that enervating grief, like trying to run in a dream, one heavy foot dragging behind the other while you never get closer to where you're trying to go.

"He could die," I said. People died at seventy-eight. This time the possibility of abandonment was not just in my head.

"He *will* die," Allie said. "The question is, do you want to spend some time with a remarkable man or not?"

I did and I didn't. "I'm just afraid," I said.

Allie shrugged. "I'm telling you, he's the one."

I couldn't deny that I had been feeling it was fated, but after learning Dennis was seventy-eight and not sixty-eight, that feeling had all but vanished. I didn't want to take on someone else's end-of-life issues, however remarkable he might be.

We stayed at HITS until most of the crowds had left and most of the horses were back in their stalls for the night. Dennis and I strolled through the almost empty show grounds, slowly heading for the car. On the way home, we decided to stop at a Japanese restaurant for a bowl of udon soup. Dennis told me about living in Japan for a year to work on a book of photographic haikus based on the travels of the seventeenth-century poet Basho.

Now that I'd decided our relationship would be nothing more than a friendship, I was more relaxed and could enjoy his company without the distraction of figuring out what we were or what we were going to be to one another.

We parted later, he to leave for Europe the next day and me to begin another leg of the book tour in two days. We agreed to stay in touch and to get together at some point the next month when we'd both returned. I could tell by the way he said goodbye that he cared too much. He looked at me a long time, cradling my face in his hands. I stared back but all I could see was seventy-eight.

12

*I*n one day I received two really extraordinary letters. One from my niece, Marguerite, the first I had ever gotten from her, which is remarkable enough if you are a doting aunt and the person on whom you dote is twenty-three years old. The letter was short but what it lacked in length it made up for in depth.

Dear Aunt Susie,

I have been sitting in the Washington airport all day long because of a cancelled flight. I have been here for over twelve hours. The silver lining to this is that I feel like you have been with me all day. I read your book cover to cover and I wish it never had to end. I laughed and cried. That's one cool thing about an airport. You don't know anyone so I could do both openly. I related to your honest writing and I was inspired by it. I love you so much and I wanted to tell you that you have been a comfort to me throughout my life. Thanks for dedicating this book to me. It means the world.

All my love,
Muggs

My brother and his family lived five hours away and because of that, I'd almost missed seeing his children grow up. Even if I managed to get there twice a year, big things would happen between visits. First steps, first words, school plays and concerts, all of them growing inch by inch to six feet or more, the whole rhythm and arc of their lives. I alternated between feeling guilt and despair about this. For years I fantasized about moving there and once even went to look at a new condo complex built just up the road from Lloyd's house. I wanted to be a *real* aunt. I wanted his children to come to my house after school and eat the delicious snacks I prepared and sit around the kitchen table and tell me about the funny things that had happened to them that day. I wanted to be the backup mom, the one who listened and was always on their side no matter what.

Instead, I got glimpses of their lives once or twice a year and felt I barely knew them. When I'd go to visit I'd stare at these beautiful strangers with whom I felt such a strong connection and try to "see" who they were in the few days we had together. My niece looks like her mother but she also looks like my mother, whom she resembles so much it is spooky. My oldest nephew looks like my father, and his younger brother looks like the grandmother who raised me, especially when he was a baby and didn't have any hair. "He looks just like Granny," my brother and I would say to each other, staring at his round, white face. These physical resemblances to their ancestors touched me deeply. I wanted them to know the people they resembled. I wanted them, for better or worse, to feel connected to their family in a way I never did.

My niece is named after her great-great-grandmother, the writer Marguerite Harrison, whom I knew until she died when I was seventeen years old. I told my niece about her, how interesting she was, how she cared about the disenfranchised of the world. I went online and tried to find all six of Marguerite Harrison's books so my niece would have a complete collection, as well as one recently written about her entitled *Women of the Four Winds* by Elizabeth Fagg Olds. I told my niece as much as I could about my own mother.

I'd told my nephews about my father, emphasizing what was good about him: his humor, his wonderful mind, his love of animals. But I'd also told them about his alcoholism and how it had destroyed our family and how, even after vowing I'd never fall into the same trap, I had. I'd told them how alcohol had devastated our family for generations and that it seemed likely there was a genetic component that made all of us vulnerable. I wanted to hear them say, *Thanks for the heads-up, Aunt Susie. Now that we know, we'll never touch a drop.* Instead, they looked at me funny and said things like, *You used to get drunk?* I'd stopped drinking before they were born so it was difficult for them to imagine a soused Aunt Susie. But yes, I told them, I used to get drunk.

My niece's letter helped me feel that even though I was largely absent from her life, we'd still managed to form a bond. I had always felt connected to her but with this letter, it seemed she felt connected to me as well.

On the same day I received an e-mail from a woman named Mary Wilson Williams. It read:

Dear Susie,
I am Mary, known formerly to your family as Missy. I am the oldest child in our family and I remember you and your family, who lived next door, very well. I haven't read

your book yet but my sister tells me it is deeply moving and I look forward to reading it.

Susie, do you have pictures of yourself and your family when you were a baby and small child? I hope so. I hope you know how precious you were and what a delight you were to hold and care for. As the older kid from next door, I was privileged to play with you, amuse you and babysit for you and your brother. I don't know how you both look as adults, but as children you were very different from each other. Lloyd was a handsome child with lovely eyes and hair that I remember being brown with a red cast to it. You were much lighter boned, very feminine, lovely looking, and utterly charming.

But it is your mother that I remember the best. Of course, in those ancient days I called her Mrs. Richards but I didn't feel that our relationship was defined by any kind of formality. She was the kind of person who could even make a horribly self-conscious 12 year old feel valued and safe. She was incredibly pretty but her beauty went way beyond her physical being. She was gentle, calm and kind. She loved flowers and treasured her garden. While I have no proof of this in my memory bank, I believe she was artistic. She certainly had a great sense of interior design and landscaping. Your home was not pretentious but nonetheless very attractive. It was warm in a semi-modern, carefully conceived way. Your mother loved pinks, creams, beiges and pale yellows. Her clothes were always perfectly matched and often in those colors, although I also remember her in a red and white summer shorts outfit. She, like all the moms in our neighborhood, was a 50s housewife. She created a gracious and very pleasant household. She was affectionate with both you and Lloyd, and I know she loved you very much. She also loved Lulie, which I think was the name of your dog. Lulie was the first Newfoundland I'd every met, and I used to think she was a little like Nanny, the old English Sheepdog in Peter Pan.

My impression of your father is not as complete, probably because he went to work everyday. He was always nice enough to all of us kids, he certainly didn't have your mother's captivating charm. She was the shining star in my mind.

I know it was all too long ago for you to have much of a picture of it, but your earliest life was almost idyllic. You were a very happy little girl. I was among those who were heartbroken when your mother became ill and died. While we knew the nature of her illness and its name, that doesn't mean that we were helped in any way to process what was happening to her and to you—and by extension—also to us. We weren't allowed to see your mother after she got sick, and we certainly weren't able to say goodbye to her and tell her that we loved her. We children didn't attend any funeral ceremonies, although I think our parents did. It was as though this sweet, marvelous, very special neighbor had disappeared into some vacuum, and we were simply supposed to forget her or something.

Your grandmother took over the household. My impression was that our parents felt your father couldn't be expected to do that. Men simply didn't. Of course, on top of that, he was indeed a mess. I found your grandmother frightening. She was very rejecting of our offers to help, I believe. Then, one day, we came home from school

and you and Lloyd were gone. We couldn't understand it.
All these years that loss has been part of who we are as a
family. We really loved you, Susie.

I am so happy to be able to write you this letter and to
know that you have been able to overcome some truly terrible hurdles. I'm very impressed by your courage and willingness to share your experience with others in this book.
We too have horses we adore. Our lives are enriched by
them every day.

Take care Susie. You have always been in our hearts.

Mary Wilson Williams.

I sat at the computer and read this e-mail over and over. Then
I printed a copy and carried it outside to the deck and sat
down and read it again. I wanted to call my brother, but I
didn't want to break the spell this e-mail had cast. It was the
biggest chunk of my history, of *detail,* that anyone had ever
offered about my family when it had still been intact.
Someone had known us and loved us. *We'd mattered.* I hadn't
known that. I hadn't known that we were part of a neighborhood, that our lives were idyllic, that I was happy. I
hadn't known that my mother liked pink or cared about gardening or that she might have been artistic. I hadn't known
that she had a red and white summer shorts outfit.

I hadn't known that Lloyd and I, that the memory of our
family, were in anyone's heart. After my mother's death, my
father's vanishing, and my separation from Lloyd, my sense
of aloneness was so complete that I took it as fact. I have only
one memory of the family next door and it is of a little girl
skipping down her driveway in a cowgirl outfit complete

with red cowboy boots. Later, when I e-mailed Mary and told her this, she said that the girl in the cowboy outfit was her younger sister, Prudy.

By connecting my family to her family, Mary had provided proof that our family had existed, that we hadn't disappeared without a trace. For years, Lloyd had shared his early memories, over and over, always the same four or five brief glimpses of who we had been and what we did and I cherished them. But Mary's e-mail connected us to a larger world, to a loving next-door neighbor and, beyond that, to a neighborhood. She gave us a context, she bore witness.

As a child living in virtual seclusion at my grandmother's house, I constantly fantasized about living in a neighborhood where the houses were close together, where the parents talked to each other across backyard fences, and the children rode their bikes and played together on small, quiet streets. It had been more than a casual fantasy; it had been such a strong yearning that it bordered on obsession. With Mary's e-mail, I realized the fantasy's origin. *It was exactly how I had once lived.* I had known such a world intimately. I had been there. I have no conscious recollection of such a world, but now I realized that what I thought I had imagined was really a memory of the first five years of my life, and those five years were so idyllic, in Mary's words, that I had spent the next fifty trying to recapture them. The search had been the driving force in my life. I had looked for a sense of community in jobs, in political organizations, in book clubs, and in friendships. The intensity of the search was equal to the intensity of the disconnectedness and isolation I'd often felt and still sometimes feel. I see now that it had always been a search for home, a search for family, a search for those magical first years.

LATER THAT NIGHT, I tried to hide the fact that I was leaving in the morning from the dogs by putting my suitcase in the guest room and keeping the door shut. All three crowded together on my bed, looking suspicious as I went up and down the stairs carrying clothes. I couldn't stop thinking about Mary's e-mail. I never would have heard from her if I hadn't taken in a horse named Lay Me Down, who inspired a book, which was then miraculously published, and then even more miraculously read by Mary's sister, Prudy. Prudy had figured out who I was when she saw Lloyd's name, and then had e-mailed Mary, and because of this chain of events, the close familial world I once thought was a wishful fantasy was—I now know—an actual memory.

It filled me with wonder, the kind that makes me think about God and serendipity and fate. The kind where I am stopped dead in my tracks with love and gratitude for the unexpected, the unimaginable, and the undeserved gifts that drop into my lap from nowhere. It makes me think that maybe everything that happens is meant to happen, that there is some kind of order or purpose or plan that I mostly can't see but that every once in a while becomes as clear as a teleprompter. *Yes,* it says in big block letters, *do what matters to you most.* When I listen to that prompt, when fear and doubt don't override it, things like Mary's e-mail can happen.

Things like Dennis Stock?

The dogs were on to my secret and followed me down the stairs with my last armful of clothes. I stood in front of the closed door of the guest room and ordered them back up the stairs. *Uppy, uppy,* I said, pointing at the stairs. Lucy wagged her tail and lowered her eyes, which is what she does when she deliberately disobeys me, and the pugs sat and stared at me with guilt-free defiance, which is what they do most of the time. Even the cat joined the insurrection and came halfway down the spiral stairs. It was four against one, and I was the bad guy. *I'm not kidding,* I said directly to Lucy, the only one who actually believed I was in charge. But this time, still wagging her tail, she melted herself flat onto the floor until she was nothing but a lumpy puddle emitting radioactive rays of guilt.

I gave up and opened the guest-room door, revealing the suitcase and all that it implied. The pugs flew onto the bed, smelled in and around the suitcase, and then lay squished up against it, their funny flat faces, like satellite dishes, tracking me as I moved across the room. Lucy repuddled herself across the doorway, forcing me to step over her every time I came or went. The cat appeared and briefly considered the best path through the brown furry mass blocking his entrance before he realized that over was the only option. With one graceful, silent pounce he landed on the other side of Lucy. Then he pounced again, landing directly in the suitcase, where he sphinxed himself onto my white linen shirt.

Now that we all knew I was the source of pain and misery, I spent the rest of the evening being punished by the gaze of watchful, blaming eyes. "I do it for you," I said defensively, "so I can afford dog and cat food. The good kind."

I finished packing and went to bed early so we would have maximum snuggle time. Everybody was clingy and insecure, including—or rather, mostly—me. I lay awake a long time, pleasantly sandwiched between the pugs nestled in the harbor of my curved body on one side and Lucy, stretched against the length of my spine on the other. Just before I fell asleep, I felt the pillow at the back of my head compress and then the tickle of cat fur across the back of my neck. And thus wedged, I fell into the fitful, sweaty sleep of the menopausal, noting the passing of time far too often on the orange digital readout inches from my face, and got up five hours later, stiff, unrefreshed, and still full of remorse about leaving.

AT A FEW minutes before seven that evening, I pulled into the gravel parking lot of Burgundy Books in East Haddam, Connecticut. It is a small town of early New England architecture clustered on the east bank of a wide span of the Connecticut River. Its colonial charm is so intact that it felt as if I had driven onto the set of a Hollywood film. Burgundy Books is a small white-clapboard structure; a hundred or so years ago it must have been the home of an affluent villager. Its present owner, Linda Williams, greeted me at the door, and I followed her across the creaky wide-plank floor through several small rooms of books to her office. "You'll be reading there," she said, pointing out her window to a low, barnlike building behind the bookstore.

I waited while she finished ringing up several late customers' purchases. I never knew what to do with myself during these unstructured moments, so I wandered around the bookstore looking at books while taking deep breaths through mounting nerves. While I did this, more and more women arrived, crowding into the small rooms. Finally, Linda was finished and announced we were to follow her to the low building in the back. The women walked in groups, talking and laughing, as we crossed the gravel parking lot. I walked with Linda and she explained that I would be reading in an art gallery because the bookstore was too small to hold an audience.

She unlocked the door and we entered a large, beautifully renovated post-and-beam room filled with paintings and sculpture. At one end of the room was a long table with a flower arrangement in the middle where I would stand. The middle of the room held twenty or thirty folding chairs set up in neat rows. It was such a beautiful space, filled with natural light from a bank of windows along one entire wall and surrounded by terrific art, that my anxiety began to dissipate. It was replaced with a sense of joy to be reading in such a place. It was the second time such a feeling had come over me at a reading. The first had been when I read in the shed at the Catskill Animal Sanctuary. It was a feeling of connection to both the space and the people in it. I have no idea why it happens or doesn't happen but when it does, I feel safe and relaxed.

The chairs were filled by women and in the front row I recognized two of my former students from Marist College. I was pleased that they had come, partly because I'm happy whenever I discover that young adults still read and partly because I was touched that they had come to see me. The reading was over quickly and afterward I took questions, which led to a discussion about writing and publishing in general. There were several writers in the group and the discussion was lively. At my favorite readings the audience takes over afterward, mostly talking to each other, and I hardly talk at all.

That night I stayed in a small motel in a nearby town. My next reading was less than an hour away, in Wallingford, Connecticut, on the following night

* * *

I OFTEN HAVE a physical reaction to a place and nowhere is it more pronounced than in Westchester County in New York or anywhere in Connecticut. They both represent places of enormous contradictions to me, appearing as one thing but really being another. The southeastern edge of New York and eastern Connecticut share a charmed spot on the Atlantic, not too far from the biggest city in the world and yet on another planet entirely for those who can afford the country club–like seclusion of gated mansions and tiny private islands. I lived in both such circumstances, first as a child with my grandmother in Rye and once for a year when I was twenty-one and stayed with my father on his small rented island off the coast of Darien, Connecticut. In both instances, it was impossible not to be aware of the surrounding wealth and beauty, and in both instances, they failed to deliver anything remotely comparable in happiness.

My grandmother lived part of the time in Rye, New York, on a private road in a big house behind walled gardens. I endlessly heard how lucky I was to live there yet in her house I existed in abject terror. Life with my father in Connecticut was the same, only sixteen years later. My absent, alcoholic father had reappeared, sober and rich, and was living in splendor on a small island in Long Island Sound. I was uncertain of my plans after graduating from the University of Colorado, and when my father invited me to stay with him and his new wife (his fourth) until I figured out what to do next I was so happy to be wanted by him, I threw everything I owned into the backseat of my five-hundred-dollar 1965 Buick Special and chugged across America. Three days later, my car died in my father's driveway in a belch of gray smoke, parked between his eggplant purple Porsche convertible and his red Mercedes convertible.

"Jesus Christ," said a man squinting from the doorway of a white colonial inn-turned-private residence, as I emerged from the noxious cloud barefoot, carrying my dark green plastic, Hefty-bag luggage.

"Hi . . . Daddy," I said to the tall stranger dressed in a T-shirt and boxer shorts and gripping a giant mug of coffee. Peering over his shoulder was a pretty, much younger woman with a silky brown, shoulder-length pageboy, whose smile revealed a small gap between her two front teeth, exactly like the one between my mother's front teeth in the only memory I have of her smiling down at me to say good-night when I must have been about three or four years old. Because of this detail, I was instantly drawn to this sweet new wife, whom I later came to genuinely love and still love as a dear friend.

Within days of my arrival, it became apparent that his sobriety was, at best, sporadic. And, drunk or sober, he frequently raged at or bullied his wife, Betsy. The first time I witnessed one of these verbal attacks, I was stunned. It came from nowhere as we sat at the kitchen table eating scrambled eggs and bacon. He said some of the ugliest things I'd ever heard one human being say to another. Betsy left the table in tears.

"How can you speak to her that way?" I asked through my own tears. Oddly, I wasn't afraid of him. I was only afraid that he would drive this wonderful woman away from us, that he would destroy this embryonic feeling of family that Betsy's presence had given us.

"She bores the shit out of me," he replied.

It was my father's stock response to almost everything: movies, plays, concerts, Betsy's friends, *his* friends, me, my brother, even being alive. *Frankly, it bores the shit out of me.* He said it so often that it began to determine the way I spoke to him. I got to the point of anything I had to say as quickly as possible, talking in a kind of shorthand, conscious that I could begin to bore the shit out of him at any moment.

His tirades continued but I stayed on. I got a job at a local tennis club as a sitter in their day-care center while I applied to graduate schools. But my real job was saving my father's marriage, saving Betsy, saving the illusion that having the pretty house on the island with the expensive cars out front meant everything was finally A-OK. I was twenty-two going on ten. I still wanted a mom and dad.

It got worse. One morning Betsy and I shoved my father into the passenger side of the Porsche while I squirmed into the tiny backseat, and we drove him to a rehab in upstate New York. A few days later they threw him out when they discovered he had been sneaking prescription tranquilizers the whole time.

Another time he was in New Orleans on a business trip when I got a call from a taxicab driver after my father had passed out in the back of his cab on the way to the airport. He told me he'd looked through my father's wallet and had found a business card with this phone number on it.

"What should I do with him?" asked the bewildered Southern voice.

"Drive him to the nearest rehab," I said. Aware that my father always carried hundreds of dollars in his wallet, I added, "And take the money." He did because a few days later, my father called from a rehab outside of New Orleans to tell me that he'd been robbed. He had no memory of how he'd gotten there until I told him. A month later I picked him up at the airport on a beautiful spring day in his red convertible Mercedes with the top down.

"How was it?" I asked, impressed that he'd lasted the entire twenty-eight-day treatment period.

"AA bores the shit out of me," he said and demanded that I drive him straight to a liquor store.

The drinking and raging continued but that wasn't all. Betsy never knew which husband she would wake up to on any given morning. Sometimes he would be the happy, carefree one and we would sit at the breakfast table watching the ocean slap against the rocks at the edge of the lawn, laughing at the funniest man we'd ever met. Other times his depression was so severe he couldn't find the energy to speak. Then there were times when he would disappear—to Germany, to England, to anywhere at all—for a few days or a few weeks, always ostensibly on business, and soon boxes would begin to arrive. Inside would be whole sets of china, dozens of electronic gadgets, paintings, sculptures, expensive clothes for Betsy, all in the wrong sizes, dozens and dozens of hand-carved wooden toys, enormous crystal ashtrays from Yugoslavia (the prettiest I've ever seen, one of which sits on my desk now, holding paper clips), Murano glass vases from Italy, chess sets made out of everything from antique ivory to marble. And cameras. My God, the cameras.

This bounty didn't arrive in standard cardboard boxes delivered by UPS. These were coffin-size wooden crates delivered by eighteen-wheel trucks that had trouble getting past the guard who sat at the gatehouse at the entrance to the rock-lined causeway across a narrow strip of Long Island

Sound that led to the island where my father lived. In less than a year, the two-car garage was filled with these crates and the Mercedes and the Porsche were permanently parked in the driveway.

My father had great taste. That wasn't the problem. It was the quantity. It was the expense. It was that he already owned everything under the sun in duplicate. It was crazy. Bigger stuff arrived. Two powerboats; a build-your-own half airplane–half helicopter contraption (the only thing my father ever built was a charcoal fire to grill steaks); two more cars (the first rotary-engine Mazda and an Austin American). It wasn't shopping, it was bingeing. He was making a fortune but spending a bigger one. It was impossible to talk to him about it. He made it clear that it was his money. End of discussion.

Finally, Betsy threatened to leave him. My father was genuinely shocked. He was cynical enough to believe that just because he was rich she would never leave. But Betsy had always been financially independent, and even though my father had urged her to give up her career in cancer research, she never had.

The threat worked and he agreed to see a doctor. He was diagnosed as manic-depressive, now called bipolar, and put on lithium to level out the mood swings. He even agreed to see a psychiatrist and for a while would come home after his sessions full of wonder at discovering that he was angry at his mother (the same scary woman who had raised me) or that he had felt abandoned by his father, who had been killed driving drunk with his mistress when my father was only thirteen. It was funny in a way because it was so basic, so easy to see the troubling elements in my father's childhood.

I couldn't believe that he'd never understood it before. But this was a man who had piloted fifty bombing missions during World War II, even though every time he got into the cockpit of his airplane he believed he was never coming back, which he claimed didn't particularly disturb him. Or put another way, he had never really been in touch with his feelings and maybe for a soldier at war that was a good thing.

The lithium worked but my father didn't like it. He said it took all the pizzazz out of life. He couldn't think. He couldn't "create." He'd stay on it for a few weeks and things would be better. He wouldn't explode at Betsy or suddenly fly to Japan for really good sushi. He'd wander down to the dock in the morning in his boxer shorts and a T-shirt carrying a mug of coffee and the *New York Times* and sit on one of the boats and read. He wasn't depressed, but he was unhappy. Sometimes I'd go and sit on the boat with him.

"I'm not myself, Sue," he said in a rare moment of confiding.

"Give it some time," I urged. "You're just not used to it."

But he couldn't give it time. He couldn't live with the feeling he got from lithium. The mood swings returned, the rages, the on-and-off drinking, the spending, the impulsive trips all over the globe. I was going back and forth to Boston, apartment hunting, job hunting, and waiting to hear whether I'd gotten into the graduate education program at Brandeis. I couldn't bear to watch my father destroy himself, his marriage, the potential for us to finally be a family again. It was the second time I'd witnessed up close that money couldn't save you. On the contrary, in the hands of someone like my father, it could enable you to act out your most self-destructive behavior.

Now, when I drove through the affluent neighborhoods of

Connecticut, I looked at the lovely architecture, the groomed landscapes, the signs of privilege everywhere and wondered what kind of hell was going on behind the boxwood hedges and the big stone pillars. I can tell you this: things are not as they appear.

I ARRIVED AT the Book Vault in Wallingford, Connecticut, fifteen minutes before the seven o'clock reading. It was a spacious store, housed in what was once a bank, hence the name. I was greeted by the owners, who told me that my memoir was one of their top sellers, as there was a horsey crowd in that area of Connecticut. I was still not used to the idea that I had written something people paid money to read. It struck me as slightly ridiculous. *Be careful what you wish for.* It occurred to me that I wouldn't have been able to handle getting published any sooner than I had, that all those years of rejection balanced out the intense shame I hadn't foreseen I would sometimes experience about success.

I had arranged to meet an old friend in Wallingford. Liz was a woman I had worked with at a small newspaper in the mid-1980s. She lived in Connecticut now and I hadn't spoken with her in almost ten years.

"Are you seeing anyone?" she asked after we'd exchanged other information.

I told her about Dennis, which was hard to do.

"Wonderful," she said.

I wondered.

But later I checked into a nearby motel and felt the acute loneliness that sometimes follows after connecting with someone for a few hours. I opened my e-mail and read one from Dennis first.

Sweet Susan,

The thought of you makes my heart feel so very warm and it ain't a hot flash. Your book tour seems to be paying off and has helped you catch up with old friends. This must be very nice. As for me in London and Paris, it will be somewhat similar, old friends mixed with exhausting business meetings. I will be near an internet source in anticipation of your messages that will make the coming days less arduous.

I believe there is going to be considerable pleasure coming up in July when we can spend long periods together walking the dogs, eating new foods and exploring sites that we want to share. Although it is no substitute for the real thing, this keyboard hug and kiss will have to do. D

The keyboard hug and kiss did very well. Maybe even better than the real thing because it eliminated the issue of where we would go from there. I didn't have to decide. I could have inhabited this limbo forever, imagining whatever outcome I preferred. I sometimes wondered if I already knew the ending and, because of that, felt no need to rush us toward it, no need to capitulate sooner than I had to.

Was it really possible that in one *year* I could publish a book *and* find a soul mate? Things like that didn't happen.

But maybe I was wrong.

13

UNE IN MAINE feels like a delirious moment suspended between snowstorms. In 1965 I had been sent to a boarding school in the hills of central Maine. I was cold for the next three winters. Nothing I wore was protection enough against the winds and subzero temperatures of January and February. The romantic side of me liked the extreme weather. Girls had to wear skirts to school in those days, so frostbite was as common as pimples among us and when spring came, well, we reveled in its beauty.

I was on the Maine turnpike heading to my cousin Holly's house in Portland, where I'd spend the night before a reading at Books Etc. the next afternoon in nearby Falmouth. I loved Maine so much I often wondered why I didn't live there. As soon as I crossed the New Hampshire border into Maine, I became almost giddy even though there was nothing special about the scenery along the turnpike. It was flat with a lot of open fields and a lot of tall, straight pines. It looked like that pretty much from one end of the turnpike to the other, all five hours of it. Still, everything seemed better in Maine, from the taste of the pretzels I was eating, bought from a vending machine at a rest stop, to the smell of piney air blowing in through the sunroof.

I'd been house shopping in Maine on and off for twenty

years. When I first began, I'd looked at houses I could afford. Now, with the inflation in real estate, I couldn't afford those same houses but I looked anyway because it was a dream that refused to die.

I was so happy to be in Maine I'd forgotten to be nervous about the book tour. I wasn't worrying about who would show up or if I'd cry or if I'd misspell *To Elizabeth,* which I'd done. It's hard to be maudlin in Maine. It was as though I'd left the angst-ridden Susan at the state line and it was the carefree Susan who was whistling her way up the turnpike.

At four o'clock I pulled into the driveway of Holly's house and walked up the back steps of her small white Cape into the mud room, letting her cat, Bernie, in at the same time. Holly greeted me in the kitchen, where the counter-tops were cluttered with the makings of whatever she had already eaten that day and the sink was full of dirty dishes. I was delighted that my visit had not inspired a cleaning frenzy. When someone comes to visit at my house, I do a military-like dirt purge that takes up most of the day, a day I could have spent writing and walking the dogs. Every time I do it I swear I won't do it again because it's exhausting and, more than once, visitors, including my brother, have said, "How can you stand things so neat? I like a house that feels lived in."

Holly's house felt lived in. She's a painter and the dining room with the pretty lace curtains in the window was her studio. Watercolor and acrylic paintings were stacked on the dining-room table waiting for frames and others were propped against walls and chairs, drying or waiting for Holly to decide whether or not they were finished. She's a terrific artist and every time I look at her work I wish our scary grandmother, who loved art passionately, was alive to see it. She would have admired the warm colors and the slightly abstract renditions of Maine and Baja landscapes, two dominant themes in Holly's work. Holly is Laura's younger sister, the youngest of the cousins I lived with outside of Boston and spent summers with in their house on an island off the coast of Maine. But for some reason, seeing Holly didn't trigger memories of feeling left out, of being different. Maybe it's because she's six years younger than I am.

I was nine when I went to live with her family and Holly was three. I remember her as a toddler, sitting in her high chair at the dinner table, too shy to talk and hardly eating any of the food on the little plastic plate in front of her. But even at three she showed signs of being an artist. Scotch-taped to the kitchen wall were her paintings and scribbles, ever increasing in sophistication, but already at three better than anything I could produce at nine. The whole family was artistic but Holly was their star, the one everyone expected to make a serious mark in the art world.

She was also the funny one, the one who could make us cry with laughter at her wry caricatures. She was the comedian in the family.

Later that night Holly and I drove through Portland, looking for the home of my copy editor, Pat, and her husband, Gary, who had invited us for dinner. As a first-time author, the process of getting a book ready for publication had been fascinating to me. The copy editor is the final gatekeeper, microediting one last time, checking for grammar, spelling, and consistency before the manuscript becomes a galley, a paperback facsimile of the hardback. The letter I got from Pat after she copyedited the book was one of my best publishing experiences. She said it was the first time she'd ever wanted to personally contact the writer of a book she'd worked on. Not that she hadn't worked on great books, but she had found mine particularly compelling.

We began corresponding and met a few months later at the home of a friend whom I was visiting in Maine. That first meeting had taken place almost a year ago. Now Holly and I found Pat's house, tucked at the end of a quiet cul-de-sac, and we were introduced to her husband, Gary, a photographer who teaches at Colby College, and their guest, Bernard. By the time I hugged them goodbye on the front porch, I knew I had made a lifelong connection to this wonderful couple.

Holly's computer was set up in the guest room so before I went to sleep later that night, I checked my e-mail and found this from Dennis:

Very Dear,

Forgive the typos that might come up because I am on a French keyboard in my office in Paris. I am still pushing myself through jet lag with varying moments of success and failure.

I can easily identify with the feelings you express about Maine. Perhaps you might entertain the possibility of us having a shoreline summer reprieve for a length of time that suits you. There are sights, sounds, and flavors that could be added to our album of memories. I feel we are both yearning for that special intimacy that comes through mutual experiences in space and silence. My guess is that missing you is one part of the venture.

Please forgive the briefness of this E. The keyboard,

small type and the right hand mouse are wearing me down.
So with only my left fingers, I send love and dreams.

D

He sent love. Did he mean the generic kind as in, in order
to achieve world peace we should *love* and cherish each other?
Or did he mean *love?* And what about the dream part? What
exactly was he dreaming? I mulled this over as I lay awake for
hours through another night of menopausal insomnia. A shoreline summer reprieve in Maine? Did that mean *overnight?* It
must mean overnight. The Maine shoreline is minimally seven
hours away from where either of us lives. It meant a bed and
breakfast, or a hotel room. I imagined lying awake with a man
I hardly knew, alternating between hot flashes and the chill
that follows, a night of throwing off the covers and grabbing
them back again, desperate for sleep that never seems to
come, counting the hours until dawn. I am a nightmare of a
roommate. When I'm alone I can at least get up and read or
turn on the television or, if it's summer, sit on the back deck
with the dogs and listen to the peepers. If it's winter and I'm
having a bad hot flash, sometimes I get up and stand on the
balcony right off my bedroom and for a few minutes, it feels
wonderful. If I couldn't get up, if I had to just lie there in a
pool of sweat because the person next to me wasn't in the
same temperature zone, I thought I'd go mad.

Couples who have known each other for a long time have
worked this out. The woman doesn't feel trapped and the
man has probably figured out how to sleep through his
menopausal partner's insomnia and nightly hot flashes.
Nobody looks at the other one in the morning and says, *God,
you're a scary number.*

And even though I was in Maine, the angst-ridden Susan returned, all because of this e-mail and imagining conducting a courtship during menopause. Courtships have never been my forte, fraught as they are with so many things outside my control, like, for instance, the other person. And now my own body had become a wild card, pitching me into uncharted territory on a daily basis.

Still, it was lovely to receive such an e-mail, to be the subject of someone else's thoughts. And underneath the deep layer of misgivings about what this relationship could be was also a growing sense of excitement.

SATURDAY WAS WARM and sunny as Holly and I drove to Books Etc. in Falmouth for the one o'clock reading. It was the kind of day that's so beautiful I wouldn't spend a minute inside if I didn't have to, and I wondered why anyone would come to a reading in a bookstore on such a day. Icy rain was no good for readings and neither was a perfect summer day.

"Everyone is *gardening,*" I groaned at Holly, as, sure enough, we walked into a virtually empty store. Even the owner of the bookstore, who had greeted me warmly, admitted the weather was not on our side. I knew for sure three people would come: my high-school friend Ellen, who had come to my reading in Providence in May and was coming to hear me read again, and her mother and father. Sure enough, within a few minutes they arrived. Thirty-eight years later, Ellen's parents looked almost exactly as I remembered them. Her mother said some nice things about the book, which pleased me enormously. For a moment I felt as though I were still fifteen and had done something noteworthy during a parents' weekend at school.

In spite of the beautiful day, people began to trickle in, and by the time I read, there were twenty or so gathered to listen. When the reading was over, the owner of the store led me to a back room and asked me to sign their author wall, which was covered with the signatures of all who had come to read there.

We said goodbye to Ellen's parents, and Ellen, Holly, and I headed off together to take a walk along the coast in a pretty area near Portland called Prouts Neck. Ellen's husband, Phil, met us for dinner later at a Vietnamese restaurant and then drove home alone when Holly and I persuaded Ellen to spend the night with us at Holly's house in Portland because we were having such a good time together we wanted to prolong it. We stayed up late talking as Ellen looked through Holly's paintings. I was so pleased that two people I cared about seemed to have made a connection with each other. It has always been my wish that my friends would like each other, that once they meet they would become part of an extended family I have tried to create. It was because of my book that I had reconnected with Ellen and that Ellen and Holly had met. This was anther unexpected gift of publishing.

The next day was beautiful again, and we decided to take a boat tour around Casco Bay. We called Ellen's husband and persuaded him to join us on the afternoon cruise. The boat was full of other tourists and the guide had a good knowledge of local history going all the way back to before European settlers came to America. He pointed at little islands or a particular cliff or an old house crumbling along the shoreline and regaled us with accounts of what had happened there: an Indian warrior committed suicide off that cliff, an American navy captain sank a British war vessel near there, a poet wrote his most famous poem in that house. At one point we realized that all his anecdotes were about men. He'd never once mentioned a woman. So the four of us began making up our own stories.

Holly pointed at a house on the shore and said, "A famous midwife delivered a six-pound baby there."

Ellen pointed to another house and said, "Tabitha Sherwood baked a fluffy cake there."

"And there," said Phil, pointing at another house, "Goodie Twoshoes sang her ten children to sleep at night."

People sitting nearby heard us and began making things up, too, and it got very silly. We were laughing hard and having just about the best time ever. That's the kind of thing that *always* happens around Holly and I love her for it. When the cruise was over, we thanked the guide kindly for his tour (wondering if he'd heard any of ours) and headed right for an ice cream stand. We sat on a bench in the late afternoon sun eating ice cream, reluctant to let go of the perfect day. Being on a book tour had begun to feel like coming full circle, returning to my youth but now with a chance to do it differently, to do it *better*. I'd never imagined this. I'd never imagined it would give me as much joy as this.

THE NEXT DAY I headed west toward Vermont for my next reading in Montpelier on Monday night. I'd decided to take the scenic route across Maine, New Hampshire, and Vermont, traveling small secondary roads because this was New England, one of the prettiest places in America, and I wanted to see as much as I could. I particularly wanted to drive through the White Mountain National Forest on the

Kancamagus Highway in New Hampshire, a thirty-five-mile stretch of mountain wilderness between Conway and Lincoln.

All day I drove through small New England towns, some with no more than a post office and a grange hall. Twice I stopped at small bookstores in towns I'd never heard of to see if they carried my book. Neither did and when I asked if they would like to, both said yes, and I sold each of them four books at cost from the back of my car. This was harder for me than it sounds and after each transaction, I felt as though I had accomplished something monumental. I was not making any money doing it but I loved the idea that people in these small, unlikely places would read about Lay Me Down, that this marvelous horse would come back to life for them, too.

I reached the Kancamagus Highway—a bit of a mis-nomer for a two-lane road with frost heaves the size of speed bumps—in midafternoon. A sign at the beginning warned drivers that there were no services and no cell phone reception for the next hour and, basically, we entered at our own risk. Welcome to New Hampshire: Live Free or Die. Still, it is one of the prettiest roads in the Northeast. Mountains rise steeply on either side of the road as it steadily climbs toward an alti-tude of almost three thousand feet. Up, up, up I drove, taking in the occasional breathtaking vista of a distant valley or peak, bumping over the frost heaves, wondering if a bear would dash across the road, or even something more exotic. A mountain lion? A bobcat? A moose? Did they live here? I didn't know but I kept a lookout, hoping for a glimpse of wildlife.

Suddenly, when I'd been driving steadily uphill for thirty minutes or so, smoke began pouring out from underneath the car's hood. Within seconds, the car was so engulfed in pale gray vapor that I couldn't see the road. I couldn't even see the hood. I eased the car to the side of the road and leaped out, wondering if it was going to burst into flames. Smoke continued pouring out, so much that I was sure the engine must be on fire. What to do? I couldn't think of anything except to stand there and watch my car burn to the ground. I was too afraid it was going to explode to go near it, to try to save my suitcase or the box of books sitting in the backseat.

It was strangely quiet. There was no one around to witness the end of my car, not even any birdsong to lend irony to the situation. It was just me standing in the middle of the road, hugging my purse, hoping this wouldn't be the moment for the appearance of a specimen of the exotic wildlife.

Ten minutes passed, fifteen, twenty. Not a single car passed by. The smoke changed from light gray to pure white and kept coming but there were no visible flames, no explosions. Thirty minutes later I approached the car, clutching my purse in front of me like a shield. I touched the hood to see how hot it was. It wasn't hot at all, so I found the release latch tucked inside the grille and slowly opened the hood, propping it up on its arm thingy. I peered inside and ascertained that the smoke was coming from somewhere down low, from whatever that mess of tubing and chunky metal stuff was *down there*. I felt girly and stupid not to be able to identify the guts of my car. But the truth was, I didn't care. When men talked cars to me—for example, when my mechanic tried to explain why he needed several hundred dollars before I could safely drive out of the shop—I suddenly developed dyslexic hearing and all I got was a jumble of words and a feeling of slight discomfort in my lower back.

I'm a mechanic's dream, the one most easily unburdened of any funds collecting dust in her checking account.

The problem didn't seem to be the radiator (I knew what that was), but I waited another ten minutes and then untwisted the cap and stood back in case it geysered. Nothing happened. Either it had emptied itself in the process of overheating or that had not been the problem. I suspected it was not the problem because a thin line of white smoke was still rising from a mysterious source deep in the bowels of the engine.

I waited another ten minutes until the smoke had stopped completely, then closed the hood and considered my options. They were depressingly limited. Wait, walk, or try to drive. If this had been a normal road I could have walked to the nearest house, asked to use the phone, and called a tow truck. But the last house I had passed was many miles back and the next one was likely to be miles and miles ahead and if I elected to walk, what about the wildlife? Ordinarily, I'm not afraid to be alone in the woods. In fact, it's one of the places I most like to be. But suddenly I felt vulnerable, a target in white linen and manicured red toenails peeking out of city-pretty sandals. I was wearing a necklace, for God's sake. *I couldn't deal with a bear while wearing a necklace.*

I did the only sensible thing. I got back in the car and turned the key in the ignition. The car started right up as if nothing out of the ordinary had just happened. I held my breath, pulled onto the road, and started driving. I climbed the hill slowly, ready to stop the car and leap out again at the first sign of trouble. It was hot and humid outside but I turned off the air conditioner and opened the windows so the car didn't have to work so hard. I crept along; thirty, forty, pretty soon I was doing fifty miles an hour. Everything seemed OK. After about twenty minutes, a sign told me I'd reached the highest point of the Kancamagus Highway. There was a nice view but I barely noticed it. I was listening intently for weird sounds, small or big explosions, the inevitable return of the problem. Nothing happened and I kept going, tapping the brakes from time to time to slow down on the now steep descent. Within a mile or two past the top, my heart lifted at the sight of a road crew. People! Better yet, men! The perfect gender for an automotive crisis. Surely they would be able to help.

I pulled the car to the side of the road next to a pickup truck near which stood a twenty-something-year-old man. "Excuse me," I said, gingerly taking steps across the debris of the newly torn-up road, "I was wondering if you could tell me why my car is on fire."

The question barely got his attention. He was busy holding an orange flag that he would lift and wave at the next approaching car to signal it to slow down through the construction area ahead. Only there was no car in sight in either direction, and no sound of one in the incredible silence that hung over the White Mountain National Forest on this hot summer day. In fact, I had seen no car in the hour or so I'd been on this so-called highway.

He shrugged. "There's a gas station in Lincoln." He exhibited somewhat less enthusiasm about fixing my car than I had expected.

"How far ahead is Lincoln?"

He shrugged again. "A ways."

"Is there anyone on this crew who knows something about cars?" I asked, wondering if I had found the only young man in the White Mountain National Forest who hated his mother. Or maybe his grandmother. How else to explain such a complete unwillingness to help a woman with a car problem in the middle of nowhere?

"I doubt it," he shrugged.

He wouldn't talk and I couldn't stop asking questions.

"What do you think I should do?" I asked.

"Try coasting," he said.

"Coasting? You mean with the engine off?"

He shrugged.

I backed away, nodding, ridiculously happy with this scrap of a suggestion, this new plan. Coasting. Maybe I could coast all the way to Lincoln. Why not? It would be like riding a bicycle. I could just sit back and enjoy the wind blowing through my hair. "Thanks," I called, sliding back into the driver's seat, "thanks for all the help."

He didn't even look at me but it didn't matter anymore. I had a plan. With the engine turned off, my car couldn't catch on fire. I'd be able to coast for miles and miles, maybe to within range of a cell tower or maybe all the way to Lincoln itself. I was ecstatic with hope. I turned the key but not enough to engage the engine, just one click to the right so I could shift the automatic clutch from park to drive and turn the wheel.

Using gravity as my source of power, I eased the car back onto the road and off we went, picking up speed quickly, well on our way to Lincoln. But the descent was too steep and the road too curvy to coast unchecked. At the first sharp curve, I stepped on the brake and turned the wheel but nothing happened. Actually, worse than nothing happened: the brakes didn't work, the steering wheel locked, and the car hurtled toward the guardrail, a thin ribbon of steel that discourages motorists from taking the shortcut to Lincoln by flinging themselves off the precipice behind it to the town lying somewhere below. Time froze and a lot seemed to happen in the next few seconds as I mulled over my options: should I throw myself out of the car or not? I don't remember considering pulling the emergency brake as an option but, in the end, my right hand possessed more wits than my head and that's what I did, bringing the car to a squealing stop an inch short of eternity.

I got out, shaking. For a few minutes all I could do was walk in little circles, taking deep breaths, unable to keep myself from imagining a different scenario, the *Thelma & Louise* ending. I was horrified at my ignorance about cars, that I didn't know how to coast without killing myself. Somewhere in the back of my mind I remembered that a car has to coast in neutral. But I wasn't sure enough to try it. No more experiments. When I stopped shaking, I got back in the car and turned on the engine to try to drive to Lincoln. I couldn't stand being alone on this road anymore, alone with this car I understood so little about that I probably shouldn't have been driving it. Ask me about horses; I always got there OK on a horse. I would never have let a horse get too hot to walk or let it run itself off a cliff. I wouldn't have stared at a horse, wondering how to make it go or whether it was safe to approach. I was in the wrong century, a hundred years too late for the sort of transportation I understood, for the only kind of vehicle that made sense to me.

I waited for the smoke, the fire, the explosion.

Nothing happened.

I wound my way down the Kancamagus Highway and in less than thirty minutes I pulled into the first gas station I saw in Lincoln. The trouble was, it was just a convenience store with gas pumps. No garage, no mechanic, nobody to talk to about the problem except the pimply teenager behind the register selling lotto tickets.

"Nothing's open on Sunday," he said when I asked about the nearest real garage.

Within seconds I realized that no garage would be open on Sunday, not in Lincoln, not anywhere in rural America. It was the same at home on Sundays, and it would be that way for the next two hours between Lincoln and my destination. I called my brother on my cell phone and described the color of the smoke, the area it had come from (*down there*), and what I had done about it so far: nothing.

"I told you a year ago it was time to get a new car," he said. "Why would you take a car with over two hundred thousand miles on it on a book tour?"

It was the kind of dialogue my brother and I sometimes have. One of us would ask a critical, time-sensitive question and the other would respond with something somewhat more philosophical. "Because," I explained as eloquently as I could, *"because damn it."*

From there, the conversation went downhill fast (no pun intended). After I realized my brother was not going to save me, I took matters firmly into my own hands and went back into the convenience store one more time. I knew exactly what to do and headed straight for the candy aisle. M&M's, a box of Good & Plenty, an oatmeal cookie sandwich oozing something white and gooey, a Diet Coke, and on the way out the door, a lotto ticket. What the heck?

I got back on the road armed with sugar and toxic chemicals, the short-term antidote to any problem. They worked their magic and in less than twenty minutes I didn't care what my car did. I turned the *Gipsy Kings* CD up loud and mamboed through New Hampshire and halfway through Vermont before I "crashed" in a rest area near Orange and practically had to crawl into a Dunkin' Donuts for a cup of coffee and a blueberry muffin.

By the time I checked into the Montpelier Inn at five o'clock, my car was littered with crumbs and candy wrappers and empty cups. The steering wheel was sticky. I'd "crashed" and "refueled" so many times I felt like I needed rehab. But none of that was enough to stop me from going to the little kitchen near the registration desk where they kept the big homemade chocolate chip cookies this inn was famous for and grabbing one before I headed up the stairs to my room.

I threw myself on the bed and reviewed the day. It was one of those *I can't believe I made it* moments. I felt lucky to be dead tired instead of just dead. What force, what guardian angel, had kept me from flying off the Kancamagus Highway into the thin blue air? And how could I explain my car's running perfectly well after its dramatic but mysterious conflagration? I closed my eyes to see if anyone floated into my thoughts, to see if there was a spirit hovering around me as had been claimed by various psychics over the years. In the back of my mind I had always hoped I would see my mother, a shadowy but still-lovely blonde floating halfway between the floor and the ceiling, smiling at me beatifically. But no vision of my mother or anyone else appeared, and I was left to conclude that it just hadn't been my time. Evidently, there was more I had to learn and possibly, I thought, taking a bite of the warm cookie, more trips left to take to the cookie jar.

{ 14 }

I'D BEEN FANTASIZING about reading at Bear Pond Books since my brother moved to Montpelier more than twenty years earlier, since before I started writing. Bear Pond Books with its creaky wooden floor and stacks of books on the stairs made me ache to be a writer, to join the club whose members' names filled its shelves. It's a beautiful store in a beautiful town in a beautiful state. It's where my brother lives with his three children, his wife, and their friends, friends I'd met so often over the years that they felt like my friends. Montpelier is my other home; it's where my heart is half the time.

My brother had organized this reading. I had been invited to join a book-group discussion the night before at a member's home; my book was their June pick. It was the first time I'd been asked to attend a book-group meeting and I feel some trepidation about taking part. A writing group I had belonged to for three years had invited a well-known local poet to join us one evening to read from her newly published book of poems. She had agreed to come, and after she had read half a dozen or so of her poems—all marvelous and slightly opaque as poetry can sometimes be—the discussion had begun.

It was clear from the first question that she was uncomfortable being asked to explain her poems. Whatever she was unwilling to reveal about herself had been deliberately, eloquently obfuscated. Her poems were both intimate and detached. Every personal question made her increasingly uneasy. A few members of the group persisted in asking questions about content, rather than craft or process. *Does this line mean you were contemplating suicide? Do you really hate your child?* After dodging several of these questions, our guest finally came right out and said she was happy to discuss poetry but not her personal life. Someone challenged this and asked, "If you're not willing to discuss your poems, why would you come to a discussion group?" At this point, our guest got up and left. I was so upset by the experience that I resigned from the group.

Now, with my own work the focus of discussion, I feared the same kind of personal questions. They had already been put to me from time to time. And even though I had written a memoir, I was not comfortable examining my motives under a magnifying glass in public. I was willing to discuss the ways in which readers identify with the book or to discuss the creative process itself. It's a question of limits; I'm willing to go this far but no farther.

The discussion that evening did not become personal and, at one point, I realized that I was actually enjoying it. Twelve or so women sat around in a comfortable family room on overstuffed chairs and couches as the conversation meandered from horses to writing to issues related to aging, dating, and death, sometimes derived from passages in the book but often not. My cousin Laura had driven up from Boston to attend the book group as well as the reading the next night, and she had brought with her her cousin Lilli, who was visiting from Santa Fe. Now Lilli and Laura were here, too, and instead of feeling shut out by their relationship, their presence made me feel like someone had my back. I was not alone with a lot of people I didn't know, far from home.

The next night at Bear Pond Books, I stood at the podium and read to a roomful of people I'd been acquainted with for years. My brother sat alone to the side with an expression on his face that was hard to read. He looked worried, intent, afraid. Maybe he thought I'd say something embarrassing. Or maybe, because he knew how anxious readings made me, he was afraid I'd stumble, lose my way, trip myself up with nerves. Or maybe it was none of those things. Maybe that was what pride looked like, a new expression to see on my brother's face, directed at me.

Whatever it was, I thought Lloyd looked vulnerable. It reminded me of the expression he sometimes wore when we were in the presence of our father—in a rare moment when the three of us were together—and my father said something hurtful or demeaning, usually in the form of a joke that wasn't funny. Or only funny if you weren't the target. I would watch my brother go silent, a polite smile stretched across the bottom of his face as his whole body curved forward slightly to absorb the shock of the words, to cushion the blow. It was painful to witness, the father who seemed to relish undermining his son and the son who couldn't deflect the veiled attack, who couldn't dish it right back. I never viewed it as weakness on my brother's part. Rather, I saw and see the great gentleness my brother possesses, his deeply sweet nature that I am sure is a legacy of our mother, the quality most often mentioned to us by everyone who knew her. My brother is quite capable of fighting on behalf of others—his wife, his children, his friends, and his clients. And he fights very capably for himself when the issue isn't personal.

Before the reading began, I'd made a point of looking around to savor this moment. For so long it had seemed out of reach—a reading from my own work at Bear Pond Books. I dedicated the reading to my brother and started. It was OK. It was more than OK; I was actually relaxed. And in the middle of the reading I thought, *This is what an ISBN gets you.*

I WAS HOME for a few days before I had to leave for Peterborough, New Hampshire, to read at Toadstool Books. Except for a phone interview with the *Palm Beach Post,* I had no obligations for three days. Between teaching and the book tour, three days was the longest period of time I'd had to myself for months. I planned an orgy of dog walking, horse brushing, cat cuddling, and pond watching from a rocking chair on the back deck if the bugs weren't too bad. If they were, I'd pond watch from the living room.

I'd have time to think about Dennis. We were e-mailing each other daily and, in that way, getting to know each other. This was a recent exchange:

Hi D

I'm in Vermont at a sweet inn in Montpelier. I'm about to go downstairs to have breakfast with my cousin, my cousin's cousin and my brother. Last night's reading was fine. For the first time, I wasn't nervous. I didn't feel like an impostor dragging people out of their homes after dinner for no very good reason. Soon I'll be home to pugs and lab and for that I am VERY glad. My car is doing funny things. Perhaps I need to bump up the timetable on replacing it.

I'm thinking of you often.

Susan

His reply from London:

Before I go to sleep after a long day mostly in a conference room devoid of air conditioning, inhabited by at least seventy staff and Magnum members, I want to say good night and let you know that I am for real and I will prove it shortly. My wish is that I will lighten your load upon my return by holding your hand and soothing you. Please don't fear the recently acquired obligations of celebrity. You have the skills to deal with it all. Love you,

D

No man had ever said such things to me. *My wish is that I will lighten your load.* I was astonished. The most expensive bauble couldn't top such an offer. *I am for real.* I wasn't sure what this meant but it seemed reassuring. Grown-up. The opposite of fake. But I had difficulty responding to these sentiments. They went so far based on so little. We didn't *know* each other. There was no question that I felt a strong attraction. I'd sensed that the moment I saw him at the Catskill Animal Sanctuary when he was with a woman I thought was his wife. I hadn't been able to stop looking at him. I remembered so clearly the envy I felt for his wife having such a partner, how sad I was that I had never found such a man and my assumption that I never would. Now he was sending me beautiful e-mails pointing to a future I had long ago stopped imagining for myself.

He would be home soon. He wrote that he would be back the following week and asked if I would like to get together with him the day he returned. I had already committed myself to have dinner with a friend but we agreed that I would stop by his house to say hello on my way. July would be the acid test. I had very few scheduled readings and, for the first time in years, I would not be teaching summer school. It would be the most time off I'd had in my adult working life. Virtually all of July and August. Plenty of time to spend with Dennis Stock. It both thrilled and terrified me.

ON FRIDAY I drove to Peterborough, New Hampshire, and checked into a colonial inn in nearby Jaffrey. I was nervous all the way, worried my car would go up in flames. I had taken it to my Subaru dealer, who could find no explanation for the terrifying incident on the Kancamagus Highway.

"You should really consider getting a new car," he'd said, shaking his head at the mileage.

I folded my arms, nodding. "I don't have time before Friday."

But that wasn't the real reason. The real reason was that I wasn't sure I could afford a new car, and I didn't know enough about cars to shop intelligently for a used one. Then I got this e-mail from Dennis:

Try to hold off on a car purchase until I can help, which will be next week. Cars are something I know a bit about. On the count down.

XXXXXXX D

Is that what he'd meant by lightening my load? I imagined us going to used car dealers, kicking the tires, and poking around under the hoods. Maybe going for a test-drive. It seemed like something that could actually be fun if I was doing it with someone else, someone who knew more about cars than I do. It would also be fun to do something that had nothing to do with the issue of *us,* who we were to each other and what we might become. I lived in dread of the across-the-table-eye-lock attached to a question like *I feel ready to take the next step, what about you?* Or (with attitude), *Why didn't you call?* Car shopping seemed safe, the perfect way to spend time getting to know someone without pressure.

It was yet another rainy afternoon. At the inn in Jaffrey, I had a large room containing a king-sized four-poster bed with a canopy. It overlooked a vast pasture in which two draught horses stood under the overhang of a big yellow barn. Stone walls snaked across the fields and, if I hadn't known better, I'd have thought I was in England. I sat at the window for a while, admiring the scene below, tempted to go out to see if I could coax the horses to the fence for a closer visit.

I love draught horses. There is a shire farm not far from my house. Shires are the largest horses in the world, with great feathery "leggings" above the giant hooves, giving the impression that they are always in motion even at a stand-still. Years ago, Jerry, a stable trainee, had invited me to a Fourth of July party at this farm, a party just for the staff and their friends and family. It was the first time I had been there. In the late afternoon, I'd driven down the long dirt approach, passing paddock after paddock of shires and shire-thoroughbred mixes. The driveway ended at a large stone house and several large barns, one just for the antique carriages the owner collected and drove occasionally in town parades. Past the house, stretching into the distance as far as the eye could see, were huge pastures surrounded by brown wooden fences. At the end of one such pasture was a long, low building that was an indoor riding facility. And right next to where I parked the car, not too far from the swimming pool, was the helicopter landing pad surrounded by blinking orange lights. It was quite a place.

Later, after a tour of the whole facility followed by a delicious barbecue, we lay sprawled around on the grass near one of the outdoor practice rings, looking up at the fading light of the early evening sky. The farm was so beautiful, so magical, with all those horses grazing in the distance, that I couldn't imagine how the day could get any better until Jerry decided to bring out a horse to play with, one of the farm's two breeding stallions, a shire named Tom.

Small, slender Jerry, weighing just over a hundred pounds, leading Tom, a two-thousand-pound shaggy black shire stallion, was a funny sight. She brought him to the practice ring, unclipped his lead line, and let him go. We hung over the fence, petting the giant face with its white star until Tom grew tired of the attention and took a tour of the ring. Several small jumps had been set up, including one in the middle of the ring that was less than two feet high. Tom decided to take himself over this jump. He got himself into a slow, rocking-horse kind of a canter to do so, and then this huge animal heaved himself over the tiny jump. He did it again and again, one time even kicking up his rear heels as he cleared it. He looked so silly we had to laugh.

Years later, Jerry phoned to ask if I wanted Tom. He had grown old by then, was no longer at stud and in need of a good retirement home. But it was not long after Georgia had died, during the period when I thought I hated horses, so even though I wanted a draught horse all my life, I had turned down the chance to give Tom a home. Now, sitting in the window of the inn, looking at the two draught horses standing in the rain, I thought of Tom and that marvelous farm. I thought that there was nothing more pleasing to the eye and soothing to the heart than the sight of a horse grazing on the horizon. I didn't go out to visit the two draught horses but I remained at the window until it was dark, watching them.

At ten o'clock the next morning, I drove the few miles to Peterborough and wandered around town while sipping a cup of coffee. It was a picturesque New England town, home to America's first public library and the prestigious MacDowell Colony. It was also the home of Toadstool Books, where I was scheduled to read at eleven o'clock.

The reading went well, attended by a lot of horse people and a few who liked memoirs. At every reading there are shoppers who get trapped into listening because they just happen to be in the store when the reading begins. I can always tell who they are because they continue to browse until they hear laughter and then they reappear and stand in the back. Customers coming and going, clerks continuing to ring up sales, and the voices of children rising above everything else can be quite chaotic during a reading. But for me, the biggest distraction is the weather, the sun on a warm, clear day that beckons through a nearby window. Being trapped inside on a beautiful day is the worst thing about teaching summer school and it's the worst thing about book readings scheduled during the day.

I was ecstatic when the reading ended, thrilled that no more were hanging over my head for a whole month. But the truth is, they had gotten easier. I was not as anxious as I had been at the beginning, and I no longer assumed a low turnout meant my book was bad. I'd made a point of asking other authors about their book tours, and they all had horror stories, from no one showing up to children screaming through the whole reading.

In addition to the growing satisfaction I felt at reconnecting with old friends and family, I had also begun to find it easier to talk to strangers; to have a brief, meaningful exchange with someone before I signed a book or to talk afterward when the signings were over. People were passionate about horses and what was interesting was that no one really had the definitive answer why, though it was wonderful to listen to all the different theories. One woman said, "I love them to distraction," which expressed perfectly what so many of us feel for horses even if it doesn't answer the question. But after a month of readings and talking to dozens of readers about horses, writing, and so many other things, I was at least no longer afraid I would cry.

{ 15 }

*I*T WAS THE LAST week of June and Dennis and I were walking up the shady side of the street in Hudson, New York. We wandered in and out of antique stores, looking for a dining-room table for his house. He was not sure what he wanted—vintage Scandinavian or country French. It was the first time we had spent an entire day together. He was wearing khaki cargo shorts and a navy blue linen shirt and a sage green baseball cap that said SAUSALITO across the front. He walked slowly, stopping often to make a point. I felt something odd. Finally, I realized it was the absence of anxiety. It was called *having fun*.

We pointed at things we liked or didn't like, reinforcing something we already knew; we had the same taste in houses and house furnishings, as well as art. He knew more about antiques than I did and could tell which were real and which were reproductions. Sometimes we held hands. It just happened. We walked along and suddenly our hands bumped and one of us grabbed hold and hung on for a minute or two. Sometimes Dennis rested his hand on my shoulder. It took us two hours to cover every store on one side of the street. Before tackling the other side, we decided to take a break for lunch.

We found a small café at a busy intersection in the middle

of town. It offered organic coffee and gourmet sandwiches. We ordered cheese paninis on crusty French bread and iced tea because it was hot outside. We sat at a small table in the corner and tucked into our sandwiches. I noticed his hands shake slightly when he picked up his iced tea. I wondered if he was nervous or if it was something else. I'd noticed it before, but today it seemed more pronounced. I decided to ask him about it.

"I suppose we need to have that medical talk," he said.

"Medical talk?" Suddenly my sandwich seemed dry and hard to swallow.

"At my age, it's inevitable." He smiled. "Instead of where did you go to school and what's your sign, we exchange a list of ailments."

Ailments? I didn't have a list of ailments, unless you counted chronic anxiety, which had been blissfully absent until a minute ago.

"Should I go first?" he asked.

"Sure," I said, putting the last bite of my sandwich down, ready to be clobbered by a lot of dreadful information I didn't really want to hear. It's a terrible thing to live in fear of illness, of doctors, of vets—of anything or anyone that might indicate imminent death, yours or that of someone you care about. I hate this about myself, this lifelong, knee-jerk reaction of horror to anything medical. But I didn't mention this to Dennis. Instead, with crossed arms and elbows resting on the table, I leaned forward to listen.

He began, telling me about a few things that were neither life threatening nor even very scary. I didn't know what I had feared but when he was done, sixty seconds later, it felt as if the sun had come out from behind a big cloud. Then it was my turn. At first I said I didn't have any ailments unless you counted mega anxiety over every little thing but then I remembered my bad back, bad enough to knock me flat for days in a row, the bad knee, the bad shoulder, the Prilosec for what was now chronic acid indigestion, and suddenly my list was longer than his. And I hadn't even mentioned hot flashes, insomnia, and half a dozen other menopause-related developments. Still, talking about what ailed us felt like we'd cleared a hurdle, passed some creepy test. Dennis seemed relieved, too. Or maybe I was imagining it. We both decided to get dessert, me a big gingersnap cookie and Dennis a slice of apple pie. It felt like a celebration. It looked like we were going to make it, at least through the rest of the day.

After lunch we walked down the other side of the street but we didn't get far. It was the sunny side, and too hot. By the time we'd reached the third store we decided to head for the car and go someplace cooler. Dennis still wanted a dining-room table so we drove to Kingston to see what we could find there. A date shopping with a man, a man who cared about shape and texture and color and who wasn't gay or my brother. It was perfect.

We found his table in Kingston at one of the big home-furnishing stores, a round, reproduction French country table, complete with wormholes and nicks. It looked like something someone had dragged in from the barn a century ago. We were both attracted to anything that suggested "barn": houses, furniture, rusty tools, ploughs, rakes, wormy wood. Dennis had this sort of thing all over his house. Outside on his front lawn was an old wooden plow from France and a rusty wheelbarrow.

*   *   *

OUR DOGS FELL in love. It happened the next day, the first time they met, when Dennis brought Ty to my house to go for a swim in the pond with Lucy.

"He doesn't really swim," Dennis said, shrugging at the mystery of a Lab who wasn't a water nut.

We were walking across the lawn toward the pond with the Labs tearing ahead of us in an ecstasy of play; they were a blur of black and chocolate. The pugs were with us, too, but stayed closer, afraid of getting trampled in the roughhousing of the bigger dogs. It was sunny and warm and Dennis and I wore hats to protect us from the bugs. Chet trotted to the fence to see what all the fuss was about and watched.

When I'd had my own horses, I would let them out to join whoever was swimming, dog or human. Tempo was such a good boss he would keep Georgia and Hotshot from running off or getting too frisky. They never actually swam, but they liked to wade in and swish their noses around and nibble at the water lilies. After a few minutes they'd wander off to graze on the lawn, staying close enough to keep an eye on the splashing sounds coming from the pond. But Chet was too young and I didn't know what she'd do if I let her out, so I left her at the fence to watch us from there.

I was keenly aware that years earlier I had almost lost a horse for which I was responsible in this very pond on an afternoon in late March when spring was in the air but winter had not quite departed. I'd been sitting at the kitchen counter watching the fading light cast a pink glow across the still-frozen surface of the pond. Four horses were grazing nearby, my three plus another young Morgan mare named Molly who was temporarily boarding in my barn. She was a sweet horse who knew better than to challenge the alpha status of Georgia. The four horses grazed together peacefully as long as Molly kept a respectful distance.

As I sat there enjoying the sight of horses on the horizon, the front door opened and Seth, an acquaintance, walked in with five of his friends. They had just spent the day rock climbing on the Shawangunk Ridge in New Paltz and still had carabiners, belay devices, harnesses, ice axes, and ropes thrown over their shoulders and dangling from their waists as they clanged and clacked their way across the room. They had brought a six-pack of beer with them. They gathered around the kitchen counter to drink and tell me about the day's climb. As I listened to them, I remember thinking that I'd never had six men in my house at one time before. I'd seldom even had one.

Suddenly, one of the men looked out the window and said, "One day that horse is going to fall right through the ice."

We all looked up at the same time and I was horrified to see that Molly had walked right out to the middle of the pond. I'd been letting my horses graze near it for a few years and had never seen one walk onto the ice, not even at the edge. I assumed that horses knew instinctively about the dangers of ice. It would have been a difficult surface to walk across so they had never attempted it. But there was Molly, right in the middle. The other three remained at a considerable distance, still grazing.

A few seconds later it happened. As if on cue, Molly plunged through the ice and disappeared. It was over in a blink. The surface of the water visible in the hole into which she had fallen was calm, as though the thousand-pound animal hidden in its depths had never existed.

Six men grabbed for their ropes and equipment, now

strewn around the room, and ran for the door. I ran after them in a kind of blind panic with guilt already gnawing at me for letting the horses graze in the same field as a frozen pond. When we reached the pond, Seth's friend Doug paused for a second to secure one end of a long rope to his waist, throwing the other end to Seth, who stayed on shore. Then, bravely, Doug walked out onto the ice and jumped into the hole. A couple of the other men, with long ropes also secured to their waists, used their ice axes to chop a channel from the edge of the pond toward the hole in the center. Another man with a long rope eased his way across the ice on his stomach and started chopping a channel beginning at the hole to meet theirs. The remaining man, Seth, and I held Doug's rope, ready to pull him out of the water when he gave Seth the signal, a sharp tug.

In a few seconds Seth shouted, "Pull!" and the three of us strained against what felt like deadweight. I knew I'd never tried to pull anything so heavy in my life and I wondered how long I could stand the pain of the rope cutting into my hands. In less than a minute, Doug's head popped out of the water. He was shouting. At first we thought he was yelling at us and we strained to make out what he was trying to tell us. But it quickly became clear as we watched her head emerge from the water close to Doug's that he was yelling at Molly. Not just yelling at her, he was hitting her, over and over again, around her face and head.

"Come on, damn it, fight!" he screamed at her. "Fight!"

But it was clear Molly wasn't fighting. Even from our distance you could see her eyes had rolled back in her head and she was in shock. Doug pummeled her, with his open hand, with his fist, screaming a steady stream of epithets.

"Live, you stupid bitch, live!" he screamed, hitting her over and over.

I didn't know why Doug wasn't in shock or how he'd kept his wits about him in water that cold. At that point he'd probably been submerged for less than three minutes. But I was shivering like crazy and I didn't have a drop of water on me. I knew it was mostly nerves but the air was cold, probably in the low forties. We were all wearing T-shirts. Nobody had on a coat.

The men chopping the channel had made good progress through the thinning ice and had nearly reached Doug, who was still struggling to keep Molly's head above water. It was hard to know if she was struggling on her own behalf at all, but if she had been, I wondered how Doug could possibly avoid her thrashing legs. One kick could have broken his ribs or his leg. I wondered if he knew that. I wondered if he knew anything at all about horses.

When the channel was finished, the channel makers treaded water next to Doug while each one tied one end of their rope to Molly's halter before swimming to shore with the other end. On shore, they fanned out around the perimeter of the pond, pulling their ropes tight to force Molly's head to stay above the water. The rest of us tugged together to guide Doug and Molly through the channel to the edge of the pond. Miraculously, when Molly's feet touched the bottom of the pond, she began walking on her own and only needed to be encouraged to keep moving forward out of the water.

Once on land, both Doug and Molly looked wobbly. I ran to the house to get coats for the wet men and to call Molly's owner. I also went to the basement, where I had a stack of movers' quilts left over from my move to Olivebridge several years earlier. I carried the quilts to cover Molly with, along with the coats, back to the pond. By the time I got there, Doug had stopped shaking but Molly was trembling badly and looked as if she was still in shock. I covered her with the quilts while Doug continued slapping her neck and yelling her name.

I ran to the barn. The best home remedy for a horse in shock is whiskey and I kept a bottle in the feed room for just such an emergency. It had saved Tempo's life once when he had accidentally overdosed on a muscle relaxant. We had poured it down his throat and a few minutes later watched his gums turn from pure white back to pink. I grabbed the dusty bottle off the medicine shelf and as I hurried out of the feed room, I bumped right into Georgia and the rest of the herd, who were waiting on the other side of the door. They had seen me run to the barn and had followed, rightly believing it was dinnertime. I was relieved they were no-where near the pond and, as I left, I shut the gate that led to the pond field so they couldn't return to it.

Molly's owner had arrived in my absence and she had already spoken to the vet, who had told her to cover the horse and keep her walking for the next twenty-four hours straight to prevent pneumonia. The vet hadn't said anything about whiskey, but didn't know the horse was in shock so, between us, we agreed to give Molly a dose immediately. Horses like the taste of whiskey so it wasn't a struggle to get her to swallow about a quarter of a cup. Then we led her to the road on shaky legs and started walking her. We agreed to walk her in one-hour shifts, taking turns through the night. I was deeply touched at what Seth and his friends had already done, but I was even more touched when they all volunteered to spend the night so they could each take a shift with Molly. It turned out none of them knew anything about horses, but they had had first-aid training related to rock climbing so that they knew what to do if someone went into shock to keep them from slipping into the inertia that might lead to a coma and then to death from exposure.

Twenty-four hours later, nobody was sick and nobody was dead. It seemed like nothing short of a miracle to me. But what seemed particularly spooky in a stupendously serendipitous sort of way was that the one and only moment in my life when I had six men with axes, ropes, and belay devices sitting in my kitchen was also the moment of my greatest need for them. At the time, I didn't understand what the bigger message was. Why had it happened at all? I felt strongly that there was something important for me to learn on that day but what it was eluded me.

When I told Dennis this story and asked him what he thought it meant, he said, "That's easy. At that time in your life you felt like you were drowning and you needed to see that you could fight and win, that what seemed impossible was possible. Not only that, you needed to learn that when you were ready, the right people would show up to help."

I admired Dennis for finding the meaning in this story, for ending the confusion I'd felt about it for years. I was happy that he understood me, but even happier that he understood the importance of signs. For believing, too, that people and events come into our lives for specific reasons and if we pay attention, we can learn extraordinary things. We can grow and, sometimes, even conquer our worst fears.

* * *

THE POND SAT in the middle of my property like a heart. It was the unifying element of the land around it and a magnet for wildlife of every kind. It was why I'd bought the house. It was why Dennis had bought the house before me. It was why Lucy was usually wet, no matter what time of year it was, because there is a section of the pond fed by a stream that never freezes. It has been the home for dozens of Canada geese couples, who sometimes have raised as many as fourteen goslings in one brood. For years it was the home of an enormous snapping turtle that I finally caught and transported to another pond far away with the help of a neighbor. And it was the home for a while of several big water snakes, whose presence put an end to my swimming until they disappeared one summer, as mysteriously as they had appeared. Someone said they left because they didn't like sharing the pond with dogs.

That day Lucy exploded into the pond like the descending space capsule while Ty stood up to his knees in water looking puzzled. I grabbed a stick and threw it, not too far, so Ty only had to get his belly wet to retrieve it. Dennis and I praised him lavishly when he succeeded and threw the stick again and again, but never out of wading range. Ty and Lucy competed for the stick, with Lucy winning most of the time at first. Ty had never played this game but he was catching on. You could see him working on his strategy.

Luna waded at the edge of the water, eating mud. When she'd had her fill of this delicacy, she slid into the pond like a fat carp and doggie-paddled, without making a sound, to the middle. There was a sturdy-German-fräulein-goes-to-the-health-spa quality about Luna's swimming. It was as though pleasure didn't factor into it, she was swimming for the zeitgeist. Still, she was a good swimmer and I loved to watch the snug beige form rocking silently to and fro just below the dark green surface.

Noche stood on the shore screeching and flailing himself into deeper and deeper water, where, if he had been alone, he would have drowned within minutes. I followed, staying only inches behind him with a loose grip on his tail, afraid his little black body would slip out of sight into the dark water. I'd never seen a dog try so hard to swim with such a small grasp of the fundamentals. Given the level of his ineptitude, he should have been afraid of water but he wasn't. It made no sense. The cat wandered down to watch from the top of the rock wall. We were all there. I loved it.

Suddenly Ty was swimming. In case he was unaware of the importance of this staggering achievement, Dennis and I went crazy with praise. I stood in knee-deep water, soaking wet from all the dogs shaking around me and kissed the top of his newly wet head.

"What a good boy," Dennis and I said over and over. He wagged his tail appreciatively while Noche screeched and Luna swam in circles, working off breakfast. Lucy picked up the stick and jabbed it at my hip impatiently, making sure I hadn't forgotten what we were here for. We let them swim for another thirty minutes and then started to dry them off by throwing the stick in the back pasture. All four dogs scrambled after it, the pugs often getting tumbled in the process. Luna quit the game the first time she was trampled but Noche never gave up, no matter how many times he was somersaulted out of the way.

"Do you have good memories about living here?" I asked Dennis. We were standing in one of the fields looking back toward the house. It was the best view, its most charming angle. The yellow-and-white-striped awning fluttered over the back deck and because this side of the house was all glass, you could see inside, including the entire span of the spiral staircase where it seemed to hang from the second floor like a giant mobile.

"Sauerbraten," Dennis said. "My wife made a very good sauerbraten once."

I waited for more, for more wonderful memories to come spilling forth, but he seemed to be done.

"Just the sauerbraten?" I asked.

"I was constantly traveling on assignment then. We were away so much, we mostly rented it out."

So he had lived here but not really. At least he didn't have any bad memories about it, no reason it would be unpleasant for him to visit me here, to come for dinner.

"But I loved the pond, too," he smiled. "That much I remember."

{ 16 }

E DEVELOPED A routine. Mornings were for work: Dennis photographed flowers for a new book and I agonized about not writing. I had more free time than I'd ever had in my life, and I was wasting it. I couldn't think of a writing project. I made lists of ideas: a book about pugs; a book about my great-grandmother, the journalist and author; a book about the pond, which would interest not one single person except the author; a new novel except I hadn't been able to sell the two I'd already written. I wrote down ideas on a yellow legal pad and then tore off the sheet and crumpled it up and started over. A book about teaching? The incredible students I've had? A book about politics? None of them grabbed me. None of them sent me flying to the computer to begin writing.

While I agonized about *not* writing, I either paced or did small projects around the house like cleaning the bird feeder or organizing my sock drawer. Before you can begin to write you need a subject. You have to have a story, and I didn't have one. So I did unnecessary house projects and wasted precious weeks, feeling worse and worse about it. I was terrified I'd never write again.

I ripped out some of the bamboo that was traveling across the lawn on the south side of the house. I washed the windows.

I fixed broken fencing. I trimmed the poplar trees where the low branches hung over the driveway. I reorganized the linen closet and answered fan mail. I had never expected to receive letters or e-mails from readers, so getting them had been particularly delightful. They said incredibly nice things but the thing they said most often was, I'd love to hear more about Georgia and Hotshot and Tempo. I'd love to hear more about your life with your horses and friends.

I didn't know how to answer these letters because all the horses I had written about were dead. I didn't know whether to mention this in my thank-you notes or to avoid the subject. I ended up doing both. When I could avoid the subject, I did. When I couldn't, I gave them the sad news. But these fan letters also gave me the idea for another book, another story of something that had happened to me that might be of interest to others. And so I began a book about having written and published a book and what happened because of it.

In mid-July I had finally begun to write and Dennis was taking gorgeous pictures of flowers. We saw a lot of each other in the afternoons and evenings. We said, I love you, which felt both natural and outrageous. I could hardly believe something so wonderful had happened to me. If I hadn't heeded the fiery vision I'd had that day on the bridge, and then written Lay Me Down's story, I would have never remet Dennis Stock. That thought sent a little shiver through me, and once again, I was grateful to the sweet, gentle horse whose presence in my life had changed my future in so many ways.

I HAD AN evening reading on July 19 at Newtonville Books outside of Boston. It would also be another reunion with two women I'd known for thirty years but hadn't seen for at least fifteen. They'd known me at my worst, when I was in a bad marriage and drinking a lot. I'm amazed they found anything about me to like and yet the three of us had been very close once. We had met in our late twenties when we briefly worked in the ski industry. Sally and I were both married to men we would soon divorce and Barbara was single. The three of us had stumbled into our jobs, Sally and I through our husbands and Barbara through a boyfriend with whom she had begun a short-lived bicycle-business-turned-ski-equipment business. Our friendship was cemented when we worked for two weeks during the Olympics, chauffeuring out-of-town sponsors between award ceremonies, dinners, and athletic events.

BARBARA HAD BECOME an executive with the largest ad agency in the world and Sally, while raising two children, the head of the human resources department for a large corporation. They both lived in jets, going from one meeting to another, while I had hidden in my house drinking Gallo, stumbling from one room to another. Inevitably, we had drifted apart.

The publication of my memoir had given me the confidence to reconnect with them. I was not stumbling around my house anymore. I'd ditched the pathetic friend role for a more productive, more equal one. Shame is a terrible thing only if it is ignored. My own provided the impetus to change. Not that I'm free of shame now; memories of the past keep me humble, which isn't a bad thing. Barbara and Sally will always remind me of who I was. They were there when I hit bottom.

At the last minute Barbara was called out of town and

couldn't come to the reading so Sally came alone. I saw her waiting in the bookstore when I walked in with my cousin Laura, who was attending her third reading. The store was filling with people when the owner, Tim Huggins, came by to introduce himself and to show us where the reading would be held. We followed him down a long hallway in the back of the store that eventually led into what looked like a large wine cellar. Chairs were already set up and there was a lectern in the front. Tim introduced me to Cammie McGovern, who would read first from her novel *Eye Contact*.

Sally, Laura, and I sat and talked as people arrived and got settled. Someone tapped on my shoulder and I looked up to see Ellie, a woman I had been in a writing group with years before. She and her husband lived in Boston now and she was a writing adjunct at a nearby college. She'd seen a notice about the event in the *Boston Globe* and "of course, had to come."

There was another tap on my shoulder and I looked up to see Peter, a man I had known since I was twenty-two years old but with whom I had lost touch. We had been house-mates for a year, sharing a house with three others, when I'd lived in Boston. It had mostly been great fun but eventually I moved out to live with the man with the airplane.

We had been children when we met, or so it seemed to me now. Neither of us had a solid footing in a career or a relationship or even in our own identities. I remember one summer I had rented a beach house on Cape Cod with a woman friend. Peter had come to visit me there after we hadn't seen each other for several years. I was reading on the beach with my friend when I glanced up and saw a man in the distance walking toward us down the beach wearing a dark suit, a white shirt and tie, and dress shoes. It was such a funny thing to see on a hot day at the beach. As the figure got closer, I recognized Peter and thought, Oh dear, he must have just come from a funeral. I'd never seen him in anything but jeans and a T-shirt, even for his job as a counselor in a mental health agency.

"Who died?" I asked as we hugged hello.

"No one," he said. "I just wanted you to see me in a suit."

That had been the nature of our relationship; Peter had wanted me to see him "all grown up," dressed for his corporate job in the marketing department of an ad agency. I remember how hard we'd laughed. But I'd have walked down a hot beach in a suit and high heels to show him I'd grown up, too. I understood all about wanting to share that with someone who knew how hard-earned that suit had been.

After the reading I didn't go to the gathering Tim had arranged for the authors and members of the audience at a nearby bar. It was after nine and I was too tired. Sally and I arranged to meet again the next day in Wellesley to spend the weekend at Barbara's house.

Late Friday afternoon I found Barbara's gray Dutch colonial on a quiet street not far from the center of town. I parked my beat-up Subaru behind Sally's Saab station wagon and noticed Barbara's brand-new BMW sitting in the driveway. I couldn't help thinking our cars told a story. I had made bad decisions and they had made good ones, and here we were at the finish line. I don't think it's possible for anyone who has spent a chunk of her life mostly drunk not to feel the profound loss of that wasted time.

We spent the weekend at Barbara's catching up on each other's lives. All weekend I regretted the years that had passed. I had missed so much by losing touch with these two women. But they had grown up faster than I had and only now did I feel ready again to call them my friends in any meaningful way.

SIX DAYS LATER Dennis and I were in his car on our way to the Poughkeepsie Library, where I was scheduled to read at 7:00 p.m. Afterward, we would "explore," as Dennis called it, finding a new restaurant to try. We arrived a few minutes before seven and discovered that the reading was not to take place in the library, but rather in the large auditorium to its right. I peeked into the auditorium from the vestibule to see a couple of hundred chairs set up in the vast space and a podium at the front. And even though it was a few minutes before seven, not a single person was there.

"I don't feel good about this," I whispered to Dennis just as the front door opened and an old man limped in. The assistant librarian greeted him warmly. It was clear that he was a library regular.

"I'm not familiar with your book," he told me unapologetically. "I just live across the street."

"Thanks for coming, anyway." What else could I possibly say?

At five past seven, when no one else had arrived, Dennis and I decided to wait outside in the parking lot. It was a warm evening and we sat in the front seat of his car with the doors open. On the other side of the parking-lot wall, we could hear kids playing in a low-income apartment complex. Their shouts and cheers filled the summer air, changing as basketball shots were made or missed.

"This is awful," I said to Dennis when minutes passed and not a single car pulled into the parking lot.

"It doesn't matter at all," said Dennis. "It's a beautiful night and we're together."

I started to make jokes about why no one had come and pretty soon I was laughing so hard I had to get out of the car in order to stand up so I could bend over to laugh. These laughing fits happened a lot when I was with Dennis. It felt great to laugh that hard about something as awful as a no-show book reading.

The truth, however, was that as much as I laughed, I was a little unnerved by the experience. It flickered uncomfortably close to the memory of all those years when, over and over again, no one had come. But on the way to dinner, I reminded myself of all the ways things were different now. I was not a child, I was not helpless, and *Would everyone with an ISBN number please stand up?*

*D*ENNIS AND I were in Bar Harbor, Maine, standing on a balcony overlooking Frenchman Bay. The hotel sat high above the ocean on a steep hillside and offered a breathtaking view of mountains, islands, and coastline. Below us a large schooner with terra-cotta-colored sails glided into the harbor, which was glowing a deep shade of pink in the sunset. Above us seagulls drifted through the sky, their cries piercing straight to the heart.

Behind us was a large bright room with two beds, a living area, and a kitchenette. It smelled slightly of mildew, which I somehow found reassuring. The ocean was everywhere—in the rug, in the curtains, in the bedspread, within us. That was why we had driven nine hours in one day to come here.

"If I could figure out a way to make a living here . . . ," I said to Dennis as I leaned on the balcony rail absorbing the sights and sounds and smells. My obsession with Maine was fully aroused. I was ready to walk through town torturing myself in front of real estate offices, looking at pictures of houses just a stone's throw from the ocean that I could never afford.

"It's too cold," said Dennis, who had been spoiled for cold weather by all those years of living in Provence. "Maybe summers," he added.

Like Dennis, there was a time when I couldn't seem to get warm in winter. It drove me to buy first a hot-water bottle to sleep with and then an electric mattress pad that I would set on high for an hour before getting into bed.

"All that radiation could give you cancer," warned a friend.

"You have to die of something," I had answered, unable to imagine how I could survive a winter otherwise. Now I haven't been cold for four years, ever since my first hot flash when I ripped off a sweater for the last time and stored it in the cedar closet along with all the others I couldn't wear anymore. To a menopausal woman, a February day in Maine would require little more than a T-shirt and a light jacket. Or lose the jacket and try a sweater—certainly not both.

But Dennis's comment about winter struck at something deeper. Would it be possible to reconcile my desire to live in Maine with the possibility of someday blending my life with his? Did the new fantasy require letting go of the old one? What about all the other habits and interests that might be difficult or impossible to merge? At our age, the challenges to becoming a couple seemed particularly daunting to me. Standing on the balcony on the eve of sharing our first hotel room, we were one big step closer to addressing these things. Or maybe they wouldn't get addressed, but rather would play themselves out, day by day, one issue at a time, as we bumped into them while doing something else. Maybe it was premature to worry about whether or not we could ever move to Maine. Maybe figuring out what we wanted for dinner was all we needed to solve right now.

I had agreed to this trip with the understanding that we would sleep in separate beds. Dennis had readily accepted these terms but now that we were here and actually faced with sharing a room for the first time, it seemed highly unlikely that we would simply tuck ourselves in and wave good night to each other from across the room without feeling some kind of tension mingling with the scent of mildew. I already felt it. I did what I do when I feel such tension, something I hate. I became incredibly nice. I smiled expansively at any little thing uttered by my companion and laughed easily and often at his remarkable wit. Slavish would not be too strong a word for the kind of golden retriever–like devotion I tried to convey. Of course it was sickening. Even worse, it didn't work.

The tension didn't go away.

It followed us back to the hotel room after dinner, back to the dead center of the problem, which we would not talk about because we had agreed not to. I was still chatting and smiling, still determined to be the world's best buddy. Meanwhile, fresh challenges arose and, with each one, the tension in the room grew. Who would decide if we watched TV? And if we did, who would hold the remote? What about the sliding glass doors to the balcony? If I were here alone, I'd open them wide to the cool night air, but Dennis was already shivering, zipping himself into a heavy sweatshirt and jumping around to get warm. I got a hot flash just looking at him, anticipating lying sleepless in a sealed-up room. Insomnia was bad enough when I was alone. What were the options with a roommate? To lie in bed, eyes firmly shut, and imagine the ceiling or to lie in bed, eyes wide open, and look at the ceiling.

Things seemed pretty grim, and I haven't even mentioned *body* image and how hard it was to appear twenty pounds thinner than I really am by hiding a certain fullness of hip inside a pair of men's extra-large sweatpants and a T-shirt that fell to midthigh with a picture of a stack of books on the front that said *Summer Reading.* I was drowning in fabric. The "short" sleeves of the T-shirt fell below my elbows and I tripped over the pants going to and from the bathroom, where I ran the tap water while I peed because suddenly I was the only person in the world who performed this particular function and God forbid he should find out.

I emerged from the bathroom to find Dennis lying on my bed watching television. That is, he was lying on the couch that would become my bed when we unfolded it. The room was sealed tight; the balcony doors shut and thick rubber-lined curtains drawn to block any chance that a ray of light or a breath of fresh air might sneak in. Suddenly, I didn't care what Dennis thought of me because I knew I would die sealed up in this room without air or natural light. If I didn't die, I would lie awake for the next eight hours, sweaty and claustrophopic. I was already sweaty and claustrophobic despite the ugly blue glow the television gave forth to cheer us.

"Are you done in the bathroom?" He looked up from the television, smiled pleasantly—unaware of the great journey I had taken from best buddy to angry dictator of a third-world country—and stood.

The couch that would become my bed was directly in front of the sliding glass doors, while his bed was across the room, nowhere near an opening to the outside world.

"It's all yours," I said, dragging the curtains *and* doors open and stepping onto the balcony. The air was beautiful and cool and smelled of the ocean and dew-drenched earth. The sky was full of twinkling stars and in the distance were lights from boats and houses. For a moment I considered dragging a mattress onto the balcony and sleeping outside. But there was nothing between our balcony and the ones on either side of us except an iron rail, and I didn't want to wake up under the curious gaze of our neighbors.

"Brrr," he said, joining me on the balcony. "Aren't you freezing?"

"Actually, I'm hot," I said, mopping my damp brow with the spare yardage from the sleeve of my T-shirt.

"How is that possible?" he asked, rubbing his arms to get warm. "It can't be much more than forty."

I decided not to delay. "Have you ever heard of menopause?" I asked.

"Can we talk about this inside?" he said.

I ignored the question. "Women my age are cooking from the inside out," I told him. "We are walking around *on fire*."

"That's *awful*," he said. Apparently this was breaking news.

"You didn't know that?" I was incredulous. He was seventy-eight years old and had been married twice that I was aware of. Surely the most recent wife had gone through menopause while they were still married.

"No," he said, putting his arm around my shoulders sympathetically. "I had no idea."

Did women in France not have hot flashes or had this man been living under a rock? How was it possible that he had never heard of hot flashes?

"What you don't know about women," I said, shaking my head.

"I'm sorry, honey," he said. "Tell me what hot flashes are like."

I didn't know what surprised me more, his not knowing about hot flashes or his asking me to tell him about them. I had been with Paul when I first started getting them and when I explained what was happening to me his eyes had glazed over, stopping me dead in my tracks. He had no curiosity about menopause, not even when I suggested he could read about it online if he didn't want to hear about it from me. *Why would I do that?* he'd asked.

But Dennis wanted to know more, wanted to understand something about *me*. The angry third-world dictator vanished, and I felt almost human again. "Really?" I asked, just to be sure. "You want to hear about hot flashes?"

"Of course," he said, shivering next to me on the balcony. "I want to understand."

I couldn't help briefly reviewing every man I'd known to see if I could recall ever hearing this particular phrase before. It only took thirty seconds or less to cover most of the primary male players in my life: father, grandfather, uncle, ex-husband, Paul. None of them wanted to understand me, or at least none of them had *said* they did. I would have remembered. *I want to understand.* It suggests a generosity that is hard for me to fathom. I was so touched that the issue of hot flashes seemed unimportant compared to the discovery that Dennis cared in a way that was so unfamiliar to me.

"We can go inside," I said, ready to explain about hot flashes, "but can we keep the curtains and doors open a little?"

"Sure," he said. "Whatever you like."

We sat on the couch and I gave him Menopause 101. The very next morning, with no prompting from me whatsoever, he went down to use the computer in the lobby, where he ignored the line of jittery, unplugged guests freaking out without their Wi-Fi, and researched menopause.

I knew because a few hours later we were eating blueberry pancakes when he asked, "Have you ever tried black cohosh for insomnia?"

"What?" I said, dribbling maple syrup across the spongy mound stacked on my plate.

"And sugar," he said, pointing his fork at the golden liquid threatening to pool onto the table. "They think sugar contributes to hot flashes."

I was not sure which was worse—his not knowing anything about menopause or his suddenly becoming an expert. Anyway, who didn't know that sugar was the root of all evil, and a surefire way to turn up the thermostat on a hot flash?

"Honey," I said patiently, *"I know."*

"But I wouldn't suggest hormones," he continued, missing some fairly giant cues to shut up. "From what I can tell, hormones sound dangerous."

It was astounding, this transformation from blockhead to world authority on the subject of aging women, all in one morning. It is the gift of the Internet, I suppose, the tool with which couples can now solve everything by breakfast time.

Still, I was not blind to the effort he was making and, in the end, that's what counted.

Soon, the beauty of the day pulled us away from the table and the subject of menopause, and we decided to drive up Cadillac Mountain. Dennis hadn't been in Maine since 1988, when he'd spent a chunk of time taking photographs for his book *New England Memories*. Since I'd visited the area almost every summer since I was thirteen, I became our guide. You never know about the weather in Maine, when the fog might suddenly roll in, so it seemed wise to take advantage of a cloudless day to see the best view on the East Coast.

Acadia National Park on Mount Desert is one of the prettiest places in America, which accounted for the steady line of cars we joined making their way to the 1,530-foot summit of Cadillac Mountain. There were beautiful vistas the entire way up, so we didn't mind the slow drive to the top. As I had already discovered Dennis's parking karma, I was not astounded, but grateful indeed, when despite the fact that there were *no* parking spaces left on the summit of Cadillac Mountain on this warm, crystal-clear August day at the height of the tourist season, a car pulled out right in front of us, making available not just any spot, but the parking spot closest to the beginning of the stone foot path to the summit. *It was the best spot.*

Dennis seemed blessed with luck in general. I couldn't recall sensing this so strongly about anyone else. The longer I knew him, the more evident his great good luck seemed. He has known heartache in his life, but luck seems to have prevailed. When I was with him, I felt that somehow I was covered under this umbrella of luck. My tendency to over-agonize about everything lessened. I found myself thinking, *It's OK, nothing too terrible can happen when I'm with Dennis.*

We parked in our primo spot and walked the remaining few hundred yards to the broad pink granite summit of Cadillac Mountain. The summit is a vast area, providing plenty of room for anyone who wants to find a quiet spot away from the crowds in order to enjoy the extraordinary views. We found a natural granite bench and sat facing east toward a dozen or so evergreen-covered islands that dot the Atlantic like bits of spiky Astroturf. Beyond the most easterly island visible, the Atlantic stretched flat and blue to where it met a sky of the same color at the horizon. It was a cloudless, nearly windless day. A couple of large sailboats left almost no wake as they drifted across the water.

We slid off our backpacks and pulled out cameras and binoculars. A couple of seagulls landed near us, ready for any tidbits we were willing to share. I had come prepared for seagull guests and pulled out the two slices of whole-wheat toast I hadn't eaten at breakfast and threw pieces toward the birds. Within seconds, a dozen more materialized out of thin air, and we were briefly in the midst of a loud luncheon. The birds were practically tame, and when I was done distributing the toast, they peered brazenly inside our packs for anything we might be holding back. They were wonderfully amusing and Dennis took pictures of them. It occurred to me that one of the best photographers in the world was taking ordinary snapshots. That seemed funny, too.

I picked up the binoculars to see if I could find my aunt and uncle's house on Little Cranberry Island. There it was, perched so close to the water that when you were in the master bedroom on the second floor, which extends over the porch below, it felt like you were *in* the sea. The house was so big that when we were younger, on rainy days we'd ride our bicycles around inside. Hide-and-seek took on a new dimension in a house that size, and when we played it at night, my two younger cousins were too scared to join in because it seemed possible to them they might never be found.

Without television, radio, or even a telephone that wasn't a party line, we invented some odd pastimes. Perhaps the most notable among them was to flush the upstairs toilet and then race downstairs to the outdoor sewage pipe, where it emptied directly into the ocean. The goal was to see who could make it to the open pipe first, human or human waste. That was before the island went green and residents were required to put in septic fields.

"There's the house," I said, pointing to the biggish speck on the rocky coast of Little Cranberry Island. Dennis and I were going there sometime in the next day or two to have lunch with my cousins, so I passed him the binoculars.

"Uh-huh," he said, adjusting the zoom. "There's someone on the porch."

I nodded. "Great porch, huh?"

"Great house," he said.

For three generations the children had recorded their changing heights on the doorjamb between the living and dining rooms. It was crowded with the penciled names of all the aunts and uncles and cousins. The first summer I spent there, I had added the record of my height to the others but when my uncle saw it, he erased it. With that simple gesture he'd sent a message I never forgot.

My sense of disenfranchisement within my own family was already well established by then. My uncle's gesture only reinforced it. I was not one of them. I was not one of *any* of them—not the grandmother who raised me, nor the grandmother in Switzerland, nor the grandfather in Baltimore, where I had spent four years, nor my other aunt in New Canaan, Connecticut, whom I barely knew, nor even my father, who had largely disappeared. It was clear to me I would have to find my own place, my own world. I understood the prisoner counting off the days on the cell wall until he would be free. I started counting from the moment I went to live with my grandmother when I was five years old. At some point I understood that the magic age was eighteen.

At eighteen no one would be my guardian, and I would finally be free to leave. I had.

Of course then the question had become, If I didn't belong in that world, where *did* I belong? Who were my people and where did they live? The search for the answer to that question had informed everything else: jobs, relationships, apartments, and houses. Always I looked for a feeling of belonging. If the feeling wasn't there, I didn't stay long.

The English Department hallway at Ulster County Community College was long and narrow and painted some dull forgettable color. On one side of the hall were windowless offices furnished with old metal desks and tilting file cabinets. Sometimes as many as three people shared these small offices. On the other side of the hall were offices that were just as small but with fogged windows that overlooked a parking lot. It was to this asethically challenged hallway that I eagerly rushed every Monday, Wednesday, and Friday morning, inevitably tripping over my office mate's briefcase, which was always just inside the doorway of room 217, so I could get to my desk in the corner located directly under a vent that spewed out airplane-quality air to begin the teaching day.

When I'd interviewed for the job, my brother had asked me, "Is there a pension? Do you get health insurance? *Can you live on the salary?*"

"Well," I'd said, trying to remember if money had been mentioned during the interview, "I can see myself, you know, eating lunch with these people."

There is no question that I often looked for that sense of belonging in the wrong places. Still, I never stopped seeking it. I looked at Dennis sitting next to me on the summit of

Cadillac Mountain and my heart gave a little *boing*. What if he was my person? What if the search was over? I knew a lot about *looking* and almost nothing about *finding*. If I thought about it too much I'd get anxious. It was scary to be fifty-six and so clueless about an intimate relationship with another human being. Babies were better at it than I was. A baby cries in the arms of a person who doesn't feel safe. I'd married him.

But what about now? Had my judgment gotten better? Was Dennis the one?

"WANT TO GET a good popover?" I asked.

I wanted to take Dennis to Jordon Pond Restaurant, which serves, among other things, popovers and honey on the lawn at the edge of a large pond nestled at the base of two mountains called the Bubbles. Before it burned to the ground, Jordon Pond used to be in a white Victorian house but after the fire, it was rebuilt as a modern brick structure and made much bigger to accommodate the grow-ing number of tourists who found their way to this charming spot every summer to sit on the green lawn with a lovely view of mountains and pond, fighting off greedy bees while eating honey-filled popovers. It was one of the quintessential Mount Desert experiences, and I wanted to share it with Dennis.

"Sure," he said, without asking for details. He seemed content to let me show him around. Besides eating popovers and having lunch with my cousins on Little Cranberry, the only other planned activity was to drive to Frankfort one day to have lunch with an old friend of mine. But mostly the week ahead loomed free and unplanned.

The unspoken tension about separate beds remained unspoken and sometimes even disappeared. We had a good time. The hotel room was so pleasant and the view so spectacular we decided to cook a few dinners in the kitchenette. The weather was warm and sunny for days in a row. We drove all over Mount Desert, took walks along the coast, and sat in Adirondack chairs along shorelines and near ponds. And we found a wonderful lobster pound tucked in an out-of-the-way cove on the western part of Mount Desert.

The day we went to Little Cranberry Island for lunch with Laura and Holly, we sat on the *Island Queen* ferry, huddled in the wind, and watched the occasional nose of a seal appear. We passed the huge osprey nest built on top of a rock next to Bear Island that's been there for at least twenty years. We looked at the receding coastline, at the mansions built on the hills above Northeast Harbor and Seal Harbor. The *Island Queen* stopped at two islands before reaching Little Cranberry, once at Sutton and once at Big Cranberry. Each time people got off carrying the requisite L.L. Bean canvas totes filled with groceries and other off-island necessities. Bikes that had been stashed on the ferry roof were rolled off and, in minutes, the small ferry was under way again. As we approached the dock at Little Cranberry, it was impossible not to notice the enormous house sitting above the harbor like a citadel. I wondered what Dennis was thinking. It was not as though he hadn't spent time in some pricey places himself. Still, it set a tone.

Laura and Holly met us at the ferry with a friend of Laura's from college. I introduced Dennis, and we set off for the house, a ten-minute walk from the dock. We decided to go the long way, by the road past the island's general store and the community house so Dennis could see "downtown." Otherwise we would have taken a path through the woods along the shore to the long dirt driveway that leads to the house. I was nervous about introducing a man to relatives. Would they like him? Would he like them? Did they like me?

We reached the house and, well, there it was. Someplace big enough inside to go biking in. I felt like apologizing. On the other hand, it was beautiful. You'd have to be crazy not to see that, not to feel lucky to be able to sit on the big porch above the Atlantic Ocean and watch the lobster boats putt around. Or wave at the tour boat that passes close to the shore twice a day, listening to the guide telling passengers some of the history of the island. I gave Dennis a quick tour of the downstairs and then we sat in the living room.

"Should we, you know, give Dennis the test?" Laura asked. She was referring to a book published sometime in the twenties entitled *I've Got Your Numb*er. It posed a lot of questions, which, when answered, produced a score that revealed what personality type you were. The dated test is replete with sexist, archaic language and notions: *When poverty comes in the door, does love fly out the window? Do women shirk? Is a husband's primary duty to be a good provider?*

"Sure," I said, glancing at Dennis to gauge if he was game. Every cousin and every guest had taken this test, usually more than once (you never knew, you might have changed) and their initials were recorded at the top of the chapter that described his or her personality type.

Dennis shrugged and smiled, willing to go along with whatever we were up to.

Laura found the book, a tattered old blue thing, and began asking the questions. Dennis answered them thoughtfully, pausing to search for how he really felt even when the question was ridiculous. He sat on the edge of the couch between Holly and Laura, submitting good-naturedly, even as we hooted and hollered at his responses.

"If a woman you dislike is wearing a becoming hat, are you willing to tell her so?" asked Laura, poised to record Dennis's answer to this absurd question.

Dennis didn't answer right away, as if the question merited serious consideration. And I guess in a way it did. Or it could. At least Dennis thought so. I learned something about him. Once he had decided to play the game, he played it on his own terms, refusing to be rushed or intimidated, or embarrassed.

When Dennis was done answering the questions, Laura added his initials to the first page of the chapter that described his personality and then read the chapter aloud. And the funny thing was, it was accurate. It said that he was confident, smart, ethical, honest, loyal, and creative. It also said he liked to be in charge and worked best alone. I don't remember what it said about relationships but the whole chapter seemed to be particularly positive. I remembered that not all the chapters were so kind. I beamed at the handsome man with the goatee sitting on the saggy couch in the family mausoleum, thrilled that this ancient ritual had revealed him to be a man of exceptional virtue. I already knew this, but now the cousins did. Soon the whole family would, as news of his merit spread.

I was impressed by how patiently he had considered every question. I could imagine him working as a photographer, waiting for the shot—for the right light, the right composition, the right balance. He once told me that sometimes he waited a whole day for a shot, and if he didn't get it, he came back the next day and the next, however long it took. It's not just photography he doesn't rush. He eats slowly, he walks slowly, he talks slowly, he thinks slowly. I'd always thought multitasking was an asset, that it was a good thing if you could talk on the phone, eat lunch, feed the dogs, fold the laundry, and go through the mail at the same time. Fast.

"What are you *doing?*" he said one day over the phone at the sound of a crash on my end.

"Cleaning out the refrigerator," I said, retrieving the phone from where it had fallen into the vegetable bin.

Later, over the sound of dog kibble clattering into aluminum bowls, he said, "Can we just talk quietly for a minute?"

I think it was the first time I ever just sat in a chair and talked to someone on the phone. It was hard. Everywhere I looked was something waiting to be done: dirty dishes, unread essays, an empty bird feeder.

Dennis is deliberate and measured. Unlike me, I don't think there's much he says or does that he regrets later. There's something innocent about the way he *attends*, giving equal weight to the silly and the serious. He's a listener, an observer, a connoisseur of the moment. Maybe, too, it's because he is seventy-eight. With age comes patience, the idea that to be idle is not necessarily to be unproductive or disengaged.

The more time I spent with Dennis, the more I saw how rushed I was, how I lived my life according to an invisible list in my head, checking off the day's accomplishments as a measure of whether or not I was gaining or losing in the battle of self-worth. *Do something productive*, my grandmother used to say before shutting me into my room for the day. There was plenty to do in there, lonely as it was. I was expected to read, or work on the rug she had taught me to make, or knit, or practice at the small piano set up in the corner, or write letters to a list of people she deemed it necessary for me to correspond with weekly. At the end of the day I was rewarded or punished, depending on what I had accomplished.

Rushing was a virtue. Get dressed quickly (breakfast will get cold), eat quickly (if you didn't finish eating at the same time she did, you were sent to your room), clean up your room quickly (so you could begin being productive), knit quickly (so you could begin another project), read quickly (so you could begin another book), walk quickly down the sidewalk with her in New York City or *you'll be left behind and then you'll see how other children live.*

Maybe I would have grown up rushing anyway. Maybe rushing is part of my genetic inheritance. But there was no rushing Dennis and, in his presence, I came to a screeching halt. Sometimes I got fidgety, but deep down it felt like the best thing that had ever happened to me.

"What do you want to do today?" I'd asked.

"Let's loaf," he'd say.

Loaf! sneered the voice of my long-dead granny. *Over my dead body.*

The idea of doing nothing was so novel to me I e-mailed my brother. *Dennis and I are going to loaf today.* A few days later I sent him another one: *I'm loafing hard through a rainy afternoon.* It felt rebellious and achingly sane at the same time. I was like someone who had just discovered the virtue of chewing before swallowing. *Wow! It makes eating so much easier!*

"I could get good at this," I told Dennis.

*　　*　　*

WE DECIDED TO walk back to the dock to eat at the only restaurant on the island but stopped on the way to visit the island's most distinguished and beloved resident, writer and artist Ashley Bryan. It's difficult to describe his house. On the outside it's an ordinary brown, two-story clapboard house surrounded by lawn with a small flower garden on one side. Inside is another story.

Ashley greeted us at the door, telling us to look around while he finished talking to a husband and wife who'd arrived before us. I'd been in Ashley's house many times and each time I was flabbergasted at the sight of so much interesting *stuff*. It was everywhere: crowding the shelves, hanging on walls, dangling from the ceiling, covering the floors so only paths existed from one room to the next. And that was before you'd even climbed the stairs to his studio, which was full of oil paintings, wood etchings, galleys of manuscripts, stained glass, puppets, and sculptures. Downstairs, included in the clutter of art, was probably one of the world's largest private collections of toys. Toys were *everywhere,* some of them, like the extraordinary puppets, made by Ashley. There were a number of musical instruments, and, of course, books. The house was bursting with books.

Dennis seemed overcome. "He's a genius," he whispered to me, almost weeping as he looked at Ashley's stained-glass windows. Upstairs in the studio Ashley pulled out paintings. Dennis did something to Ashley that he'd done to me once. He does it when he is moved beyond words. He stepped close and cradled one side of Ashley's face in his hand. I'm not sure how Ashley felt about being touched that way, but I do know that Dennis meant it as a gesture of great admiration. Later, he and Dennis agreed to exchange work and

Dennis selected a large oil painting of a garden that featured sunflowers, the first oil painting Dennis has ever owned.

The week in Maine flew by. The fall semester would begin soon and Dennis had to get ready for two photography shows, one in Woodstock and one in Ohio. The past week had been the best trip I'd ever taken with a man. If the acid test of a relationship was traveling together, we'd passed with flying colors. Except for the initial tension I'd felt about sleeping arrangements, there hadn't been an uncomfortable moment.

We unloaded his car at his house and before I got into mine to drive back to Olivebridge, we said goodbye in his driveway.

"It was like spending a week with my best friend," I said, hugging him hard.

He put his hands on my shoulders and pushed me away a little so he could look into my eyes. "I don't want a best friend," he said gently.

For a moment I was confused. Did this mean he didn't like me?

"I would like you to be a partner in *all* ways," he continued. "But I cannot *just* be your friend."

Sex. He was talking about sex. The elephant in the room was finally being acknowledged. Worse, it seemed to be in danger of stampeding, flattening everything in its path. But suddenly I was more angry than afraid.

"I told you I'm not interested in a partner," I reminded him, pulling away from his grip on my shoulders. "And I meant it."

I'd thought about this for weeks: what kind of relationship I wanted, how I wanted it to be. I'd decided that if Dennis was to be in my future, it would have to be as a friend, as a cherished companion. I was no longer interested in a full-time partner. I was too old, too independent, too, well—I felt too unsexy.

"Then I'm sorry," he said. "I can't continue this."

The stampede was over fast but the destruction had been total.

"Neither can I," I said. Anger kept me strong, kept me deadly.

"Then goodbye," he said.

He turned to walk into the house but before he did, I could see that he was crying.

I was too angry to cry. Too numb to do anything but walk to my car and get in. I watched him go through his front door and shut it behind him.

He was not the kind of person who would call me up later and say, *What was I thinking? I've changed my mind.* And neither was I.

It was over. Just like that.

On the way home I tried to assess the damage. How bad would the fallout be? Once the adrenaline rush was over, once I was no longer numb with shock, how big would this loss feel? Would it matter a lot or a just a little? As I drove across the Ashokan Reservoir, I thought about all the years I'd lived alone, all the years I'd lived without Dennis Stock, and I knew I'd be OK. I'd miss him but I finally knew for sure that a partner wasn't right for me. Not in this lifetime. I was someone who was meant to be alone. I could bear loneliness. I'd been doing it all my life.

{ 18 }

I BELIEVE IN SIGNS. I don't know what religion that is or if it's any religion at all, but I particularly believe in animal auguries: seeing any kind of animal in quantity means something significant, something good.

On the way home from Dennis Stock's house that day in late August, the day we so abruptly parted company, I was halfway across the Ashokan Reservoir when a bald eagle flew less than ten feet above my open sunroof. *See,* a voice within me said as clear as the swoosh of his wings, *I am as free and as strong as this eagle. I am meant to soar alone.*

A few days later, crossing the same reservoir, a pair of bald eagles flew just above my sunroof and I heard that same voice say, *WHAT?*

I had no choice but to pay attention. It was unusual enough to spot one bald eagle. But two? Two birds. A pair. A couple. Mated for life. Perhaps seeing just the one eagle a few days earlier had actually been a sign to pay attention, a reminder to me to keep looking for my life partner.

So that very day, with sweaty palms and a pounding heart, I picked up the phone and called Dennis.

"Were you ever going to call me again?" I asked, less afraid of his answer than I might have been because I had seen the eagles and there had been two.

"Probably," he said, too casually.

It didn't sound like he was suffering much. But what did it matter? It was settled. The animals had spoken. It was no longer in our hands.

ON A WARM October evening, Friday the thirteenth, 2006, I was at the opening of Dennis's show at Studio B in Woodstock. It was entitled *Dennis Stock Goes to Hollywood,* and featured some of his most famous photographs of actors and directors. The show had been coordinated with the Woodstock Film Festival. The opening night drew a large crowd of both film buffs and people in the industry. Dennis looked elegant in a black shirt and black silk pants. Half the people came in jeans and half were dressed to the nines. I was on the dressy side in black pants and a red silk shirt with a mandarin collar. And Dennis and I were together because, of course, the eagles had been right.

For three hours the gallery was packed with people sipping wine and nibbling cheese as they looked at young Audrey Hepburn being directed by Billy Wilder or John Wayne carrying a fake horse over his shoulder across a dusty field or James Dean standing fondly next to a hog on his farm in Indiana. Most of the shots were informal, and always framed the subject in a sympathetic moment. Dennis's guiding artistic principle has always been to celebrate the subject, to capture what is best in him or her. My favorite was of Marilyn Monroe sitting on top of a stepladder watching another actor work. She looks childlike and vulnerable, like someone you'd want to protect.

This opening seemed like the most glamorous party ever. All night, people I knew came by, in addition to the film

people who were everywhere. They were easy to spot because
they were either flamboyantly gay, outrageously overdressed,
classically underdressed, or had really cool eyeglasses you
wouldn't find in the mall. These people were not afraid of
mousse and used whatever it took to make hair look spiky. And
they were movie-star thin whether they were actors or not.

After the show, we went to a dinner party at a restaurant.
In the middle of dessert, Gretchen, at one end of the long
table, shouted to Dennis at the other, "So, Dennis, what are
your intentions toward my friend Susan?"

And without looking up from his apple pie, Dennis
shouted back, "I'm going to marry her!"

It was a strange way to hear the M-word for the first time.
"Dennis!" I said, smiling gamely.

"When?" shouted Gretchen.

"As soon as possible," he shouted back.

"Darling, shouldn't you have mentioned this to me first?" I
hissed into his ear.

He nodded toward Gretchen. "She asked, and I answered."

ON FRIDAY, DECEMBER 22, I walked around the house
cautiously, taking my time feeding the dogs and cat. I
changed the water in the dog's bowl and carried it back to
its spot by the back door ever so slowly, careful not to spill
a drop. When I was done, I wiped around the kitchen sink
and gave the counters one more swipe even though they'd
been spotless for hours. On the windowsill above the sink
was a single large sunflower in a blue ceramic pitcher. As I
wandered around the house, I checked the corners for dust
bunnies, for clumps of dog hair that blew around the floor
like tumbleweeds. I straightened the scatter rugs that the

dogs had scrunched up, running around corners too fast, chasing the cat or each other, or looking for me as I wandered around the house.

I am getting married at one o'clock, I told myself.

If I thought about it too much, I wouldn't go through with it. I'd been terrified for weeks, ever since Dennis had brought it up at the dinner party the night of his photography show opening. I wanted to marry him. One way or another, I knew we'd be together because I'd seen the eagles and animals don't lie. Not in my religion. And from the very beginning there'd been that sense of predestination.

Still, I was terrified, so terrified that I'd made Dennis promise a number of things: no guests, no party, no gifts (not even a card), no wedding rings, no flowers, no *fuss.* We would have the smallest, quickest, most innocuous ceremony in front of a justice of the peace at city hall and our witnesses would be anyone who happened to be walking by. He agreed to all my terms. And then slowly, quietly, with the stealth of a pug eating out of the kitchen garbage can in the middle of the night, he sneaked in a few changes.

That's why I was wandering around the house in a quiet state of shock, adjusting picture frames and puffing up couch pillows. Actually, he'd broken every single promise. People were coming, flowers were already here, presents and cards had arrived, and there had been a lot of fussing to arrange everything. I myself had done practically nothing save for picking up the phone to invite Dorothy, the one person I was not embarrassed to have witness my all-day anxiety attack. Dennis had invited Andrea, because she is his best friend, and also a professional photographer. Then

Doug called, also a professional photographer, and someone Dennis really loves and *Well, honey,* he said with his hand over the phone, *he and his wife are so wonderful, let's have them, too.* So Doug and Theresa were coming, and *Honey, what about Charlie? I can't get married without Charlie.* So someone from Ohio named Charlie was coming and then there was Kevin, the man who was going to marry us. To me it was a *mob.* It might as well have been a sit-down wedding for two hundred at the Plaza Hotel.

We'd even selected wedding rings. On my birthday, December 12, Dennis had persuaded me to accompany him to New York City, where he had to attend a business meeting at Magnum. He'd spent one day at his meeting but the next day he designated as ring-shopping day, and we headed for the diamond district. I'd never been to the diamond district of New York, so it was an eye-opening experience.

At one end of West Forty-seventh Street, there are two enormous diamond-shaped streetlights marking the entrance to the glitziest block in Manhattan. The block is jammed with people staring into shopwindows filled with diamonds. There is a carnival feel, a wheeler-dealer feel, a someone-is-spending-a-lot-of-money feel in the air. We wandered in and out of shops, assaulted by sellers hawking diamonds like carnival rides. There is no question that diamonds are beautiful. But the more I looked at them, the more I realized I couldn't own a diamond ring. I couldn't own something that had left a trail of suffering behind it. So what did I want? What was I looking for? I had no idea but continued to look, hoping I'd know it when I saw it.

By the end of the morning, we'd gone into every store on

one side of the street, and I was sick and tired of looking at rings. "It's OK," I said to Dennis. "I don't need a ring anyway. Let's leave." He hadn't complained once about my indecision, about the dozens of rings I had tried on and taken off, shaking my head, No, not this one. Not that one. Not any of them. How could anyone choose one ring out of millions? It was too much for me, and I couldn't stand my feeling that Dennis was bored to death by it all.

He suggested we go to lunch and come back in the afternoon. "We need to be patient," he said. "We'll look until we find it. We need to go into every store."

Every store? I was touched by his willingness to hang over my shoulder for another three hours while I hemmed and hawed. I had never been so *indulged.* It was so wonderful that I fell in love with him all over again, right in the middle of West Forty-seventh Street. After lunch, we started on the opposite side of the street and wove in and out of stores again, barely escaping the clutches of the most aggressive salespeople I'd ever seen. They'd come out from behind the counter and reach for your elbow. "Let me show you . . ."

Sometimes you walked through a door and there were half a dozen different stores inside. That's how we found Firenze Jewels. It was a little shop inside a big building full of jewelers' stalls. Nobody grabbed my elbow when we walked by the counter. Nobody said I'd need at least seven karats to be happy. We were free to bend over the jewelry showcase and study a row of modest-looking rings.

"That one," I said, pointing to a gold ring with an oval-shaped yellow solitaire.

"It's a citrine," said the store owner, taking it out of the case and handing it to me.

"I like it," said Dennis when I slipped it on and held up my hand.

"Me, too," I said.

"Me, too," said the owner.

And that's how we found my wedding ring.

Then I learned that the building at 15 West Forty-seventh Street where we bought my ring used to be where Magnum had its offices. Honest. Another sign?

Dennis bought a ring, too. He'd seen one he liked while we were looking for mine, so after we were finished at Firenze Jewels, we walked a few stores up the street and Dennis got a wedding band, too.

WE WOULD BE getting married in half an hour. I heard the doorbell ring. Dennis went to answer it, and then I hear him laughing, so I went to investigate, and there was someone wearing a giant penguin head. We were both on edge about the big day, so it didn't take much to push us over, and this did it. We laughed so hard we had to hold onto the wall. Andrea, who knew we might be feeling tense, had found a good way to lighten things up. The others arrived soon afterward and I met Dennis's friend Charlie for the first time. I liked him instantly and was glad Dennis had persuaded me to let him come. When we were all assembled, all eight of us, Kevin gathered us together in the living room for the short ceremony. We had decided to get married in the house so the animals could come, so we made sure they were all present before Kevin read the standard wedding vows. The only thing we added was something Dennis had used in one of his books, *Brother Sun,* a celebration of life called *The Canticle of the Sun* by St. Francis of Assisi. We asked Kevin to read the first eight stanzas.

Most high, all powerful, all good Lord! All praise is yours, all glory, all honor, and all blessing. To you, alone, Most High, do they belong. No mortal lips are worthy to pronounce your name.

Be praised, my Lord, through all your creatures, especially through my lord Brother Sun, who brings the day; and you give light through him. And he is beautiful and radiant in all his splendor! Of you, Most High, he bears the likeness.

Be praised, my Lord, through Sister Moon and the stars; in the heavens you have made them, precious and beautiful.

Be praised, my Lord, through Brothers Wind and Air, and clouds and storms, and all the weather, through which you give your creatures sustenance.

Be praised, my Lord, through Sister Water; she is very useful, and humble, and precious, and pure.

Be praised, my Lord, through Brother Fire, through whom you brighten the night. He is beautiful and cheerful, and powerful and strong.

Be praised, my Lord, through our sister Mother Earth, who feeds us and rules us, and produces various fruits with colored flowers and herbs.

Be praised, my Lord, through those who forgive for love of you; through those who endure sickness and trial. Happy those who endure in peace, for by you, Most High, they will be crowned.

We exchanged rings and Kevin said, "I now pronounce you husband and wife."

Suddenly, for the first time in weeks, I could breathe normally. The wait was over—the feared moment, the terrible unknown, the big trap, the whatever I had imagined was over, and I snapped out of the semicoma I'd been in for weeks.

"I'm *married*," I said, squeezing Dennis in a bear hug.

"So am I," he said, squeezing me back.

"What a *coincidence*," I said.

And for the first time in longer than I can remember, my heart was filled with pure, uncomplicated joy.

I CANNOT RESIST connecting the dots in my life. It is more an exercise of gratitude rather than one of merely tracing a path because I have not gotten here alone. Perhaps it would be possible to go all the way back to the house in Loudon Woods in Rye, back to the disintegration of my family, and connect every dot that eventually led me to this year in which I have found such personal and professional joy. And maybe sometime I'll do that, just for the fun of it.

But what feels more honest, what feels certain, is that what changed my life most profoundly and set it on a trajectory I could not have foreseen was a horse named Lay Me Down. From the moment she stumbled into my life in the muddy paddock of the SPCA in 1992, she forced me to grow in ways I didn't know were possible for me. She forced me to change. Rather, love forced me to change. A love like hers cast a light so strong it was impossible not to reach toward its brightness. It was impossible not to respond. She gave no hint of the suffering she had endured. Neither of us had a past anyone would want but only Lay Me Down was free of it. It was a lesson I needed to learn and the universe provided the perfect being to teach me and inspire me.

I honored her in the only way I knew. I wrote a book about her. And the book sold. And Soho sent me on a book tour. And on that tour, I rebuilt a family from the ashes of the one I had lost. And I met my beloved Dennis. And I got married. And that's where the dots have led so far, and I am truly happy at last.

In the living room at Dennis's house the day of our wedding.

ACKNOWLEDGMENTS

Once again I would like to thank my agent, the wonderful Helen Zimmermann, for being a thoughtful, intelligent, and often humorous guide through the business side of book publishing. Thank you, Helen, for getting us to places I never dreamed we'd go.

I would also like to thank my editor and publisher at Soho Press, Laura Hruska, for her extensive collaboration on this book and for giving me the kind of editing experience writers are told doesn't exist anymore but one every author hopes against hope she will find anyway. I found it in Laura and I am deeply grateful.

I don't think I would still be writing if it weren't for my friend and independent editor, Nan Satter, who believed in me at a time when no one else did. Thank you, Nan, for making me a better writer and for always giving me a reason to hope no matter what the rejection letters said!

I want to give a special thanks to Maureen Brady, whose writing workshop gave me the courage and the tools to begin. Every nascent writer should have someone as supportive as Maureen to commence her writing journey.

And if Maureen helped me to begin writing, it was Susan Brown who kept me going. Thank you, Susan, for your valuable classes, editing, and encouragement. But mostly thank you for your wisdom and understanding about what is and isn't truth.

And once again, I would like to thank my brother, Lloyd, for his love and support. I cannot imagine going through life without you.